Korea 1951–53

US Soldier
VERSUS
Chinese Soldier

COMBAT

Chris McNab

Illustrated by Adam Hook

OSPREY PUBLISHING
Bloomsbury Publishing Plc
Kemp House, Chawley Park, Cumnor Hill, Oxford OX2 9PH, UK
29 Earlsfort Terrace, Dublin 2, Ireland
1385 Broadway, 5th Floor, New York, NY 10018, USA
E-mail: info@ospreypublishing.com
www.ospreypublishing.com

OSPREY is a trademark of Osprey Publishing Ltd

First published in Great Britain in 2022

A catalog record for this book is available from the British Library.

ISBN: PB 9781472845320; eBook 9781472845337;
ePDF 9781472845306; XML 9781472845313

22 23 24 25 26 10 9 8 7 6 5 4 3 2 1

Maps by www.bounford.com
Index by Rob Munro
Typeset by PDQ Digital Media Solutions, Bungay, UK
Printed and bound in India by Replika Press Private Ltd.

Osprey Publishing supports the Woodland Trust, the UK's leading
woodland conservation charity.

To find out more about our authors and books visit
www.ospreypublishing.com. Here you will find extracts, author
interviews, details of forthcoming events and the option to sign up for
our newsletter.

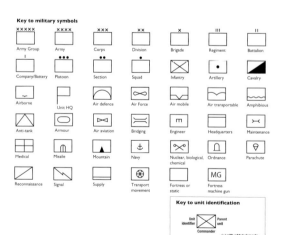

CONTENTS

Introduction

The Korean War (1950–53) has long been regarded as "the forgotten war" of the 20th century. World War II and the Vietnam War are universally known, even among those with almost no interest in military history. The Korean War, by contrast, sits in the valley between these two peaks, hidden in the shadows of the towering conflicts either side. This should not be the case. Fought at the confluence of immense and important strategic, political, and military currents, the Korean War was the first major combat expression of the Cold War. In Europe, Soviet-style communism and Western-style democratic capitalism postured over the new ideological and physical borders drawn in the wake of Germany's defeat in 1945. Thankfully, no superpower shots were fired there. In Korea, by contrast, a US-led multinational army, which at the war's peak involved forces from 21 nations under the United

This photograph of a typical Korean landscape gives a sense of the offensive and defensive challenges posed by topography. The renowned US Army commander and historian, Brigadier General S.L.A. Marshall, described the "vastness and perversity of the ridge-ribbed countryside" of Korea, meaning that "no element could be kept in a normal or practical working alignment with anything else" (Marshall 1951: 58). (American Newspapers/Gado/Getty Images)

Lieutenant General Matthew B. Ridgway (front row, left) was a galvanizing force in the Korean War when he took over command of the Eighth US Army in Korea (EUSAK) on December 23, 1950. He had a notable habit of wearing hand grenades at chest level, earning him the nicknames "Old Iron Tits" and "Tin Tits." (US Army/Wikimedia/Public Domain)

Nations (UN) umbrella, fought both North Korea and communist China in outright conventional warfare for three years. The aggregated military and civilian casualties from this conflict are dreadful estimates at best, but 3–4.5 million dead is not unrealistic, the death toll including 35,574 US and *c.*300,000 Chinese troops. The bulk of the death toll, however, fell on Korea's unfortunate civilians.

The combat in this theater was, for the United States especially, a new type of warfare, stretching and mutating the tactical doctrines that had been developed so recently in World War II. The actions ranged from great conventional campaigns of movement by armies, corps, and divisions through to scrappy small-unit clashes around rock-hewn mountainous positions at high

This rare photograph taken at a front-line command post depicts three of the masterminds of Chinese strategy and tactics during the Korean War, from left to right: Chen Geng, Peng Dehuai, and Deng Hua. (People's Republic of China Ministry of Culture/Wikimedia/Public Domain)

Private First Class Julius Van Den Stock of the US Army's Co. A, 32d RCT (7th Infantry Division), rests on a Chinese bunker after its capture in April 1951. Captured weapons here are a Soviet 7.62mm Degtyaryov DP light machine gun and RPG-43 hand-held antitank grenade, the latter a heavy and awkward weapon to use effectively. (Sgt. Bobby Bethune/NARA/Wikimedia/ Public Domain)

altitudes. As in World War II, a new generation of US soldiers found themselves fighting for their lives a very long way from home, in surroundings utterly foreign to them, their locations often unnamed on maps until conflict required their operational labeling. Although, thankfully, the Korean War never became the atomic conflict that at one point it threatened to become, it nevertheless defined political and strategic relations in Southeast Asia to the present day.

The specific focus of this book is the fight between US and Chinese forces following the Chinese intervention in November 1950 (see p.8 for details). The US and Chinese armies of the early 1950s differed in almost every conceivable way – ideology, personal equipment, weaponry, logistics, tactics, command and control, and much more. China's People's Liberation Army (PLA) was, at least in the first years of the war, a communist revolutionary force in nature, albeit one with extensive experience of conventional warfare (against both the Chinese nationalists and the Japanese). The US Army, by contrast, was a true military superpower, emerging from the recent cauldron

of World War II as the most technologically and industrially advanced of the world's armies. As such, the struggle between these two forces was a battle of system and belief as much as conventional tactics, each side exhibiting its own combination of strengths and weaknesses.

This photograph of early-war PVA troops shows the diversity of kit and equipment prevalent in the growing Chinese armed forces. The machine-gunner on the left of the front row has a Japanese 6.5mm Type 11 light machine gun while his comrades to his left are mainly armed with the American 9mm M42 submachine gun, small numbers of which had been channeled into Chinese resistance hands during the Japanese occupation. (Bettmann/Getty Images)

Close air support (CAS) was a clear advantage held by the US forces over the PVA. Here a US Air Force B-26B Invader of the 452d Bombardment Wing hits a target with napalm in North Korea. (USAF/US National Archive/ Wikimedia/Public Domain)

The Korean peninsula was a particularly unforgiving setting for the titanic struggle that unfolded in 1950–53. Terrain and climate have a governing effect on any military campaign, but in Korea environmental factors were so significant that they almost take combatant status. The Korean peninsula, framed between the Yellow Sea to the west and the Sea of Japan to the east, is approximately 680 miles from north to south and 186 miles from east to west. While there are open plains in this long, narrow landmass, mainly concentrated in the south and the west, much of the peninsula is dominated by the mountain chains that run its length. Movement through this landscape, especially in the 1950s, was often a grindingly slow business, punishing for humans, animals, and vehicles. Elevated terrain was frequently negotiable only via precarious, crumbling gravel tracks; ice, snow, and rain added to the misery of movement and endurance. Valleys snaked through the mountains and offered natural avenues of movement, but during the conflict they became highly contested routes, vulnerable to ambush from the slopes above, while they also baked under the sun in summer and froze hard in the winter. In this terrain, and also in Korea's forests, villages, towns, and cities, hundreds of thousands of soldiers met in combat between 1950 and 1953.

The People's Republic of China's entry into the war in November 1950 was a shocking slap in the face for US and United Nations Command (UNC) forces. The war had begun on June 25, 1950, when the communist North Korean People's Army (NKPA) surged across the 38th Parallel into the US-backed southern Republic of Korea (ROK; also known as South Korea). North Korea was seeking the military option to reunite the peninsula, which had been temporarily divided into North and South after the defeat of Japan in 1945. For the first three months, the fall of South Korea to the communists was a very real possibility. ROK troops, limited US forces of "Task Force Smith," then (from July 1950) the Eighth United States Army in Korea (EUSAK), were squeezed back into a beleaguered pocket of resistance behind the "Pusan Perimeter" in the far southeastern corner of the country. Through a nail-biting mobile defense, the US and, increasingly, UN forces held on, their strength growing. Then General of the Army Douglas MacArthur – US Army Commander-in-Chief, Far East (CINCFE) and Commander-in-Chief UN Command (CINCUNC) – launched his game-changing amphibious invasion behind enemy lines at Inchon in September 1950, triggering the breakout from the Pusan Perimeter and a mighty US-led advance, driving the NKPA northward. UNC forces were crossing the 38th Parallel by October 7 and by the end of the month were pressing up toward the Yalu River, which formed the border between the People's Republic of China and Korea, having driven through much of North Korea.

The People's Republic of China was at this point only a year old, born out of the recent Communist victory over the Nationalists following two decades of civil war. In October and November 1950, the Chinese leadership under Mao Zedong, alarmed at the prospect of the United States taking communist North Korea and potentially crossing the border into the People's Republic of China, unleashed soldiers of the People's Volunteer Army (PVA), a politically pragmatic relabeling of troops from the national People's Liberation Army (PLA), over the Yalu River into North Korea. It was the beginning of three years of warfare between Chinese and US forces. The offensive was of such scale and ferocity that once again US and UN forces were driven back across the 38th Parallel. The Korean War, already an international conflict, had dramatically widened in both its scope and significance.

Three key differences between the two armies were training, weaponry, and tactics, which diverged on almost every level. Given the disparity in these key areas, one might expect repeatedly one-sided outcomes on the battlefield. As the three battlefield studies in this book will show, however, ultimately neither side was able to achieve a convincing dominance over the other. This book focuses on three specific engagements fought between these two opponents: Chipyong-ni (1951), Triangle Hill (1952), and Pork Chop Hill (1953). Taken together, these battles are of compelling interest at both the tactical and operational levels. The period from late 1950 until war's end in July 1953 saw a profound change in the nature of the conflict, from open maneuver warfare to the static "War of the Outposts," localized battles over scraps of rocky territory, fought with astonishing levels of human and tactical struggle. What the analysis of each of these battles will show is just how much the Korean War deserves to be remembered fully.

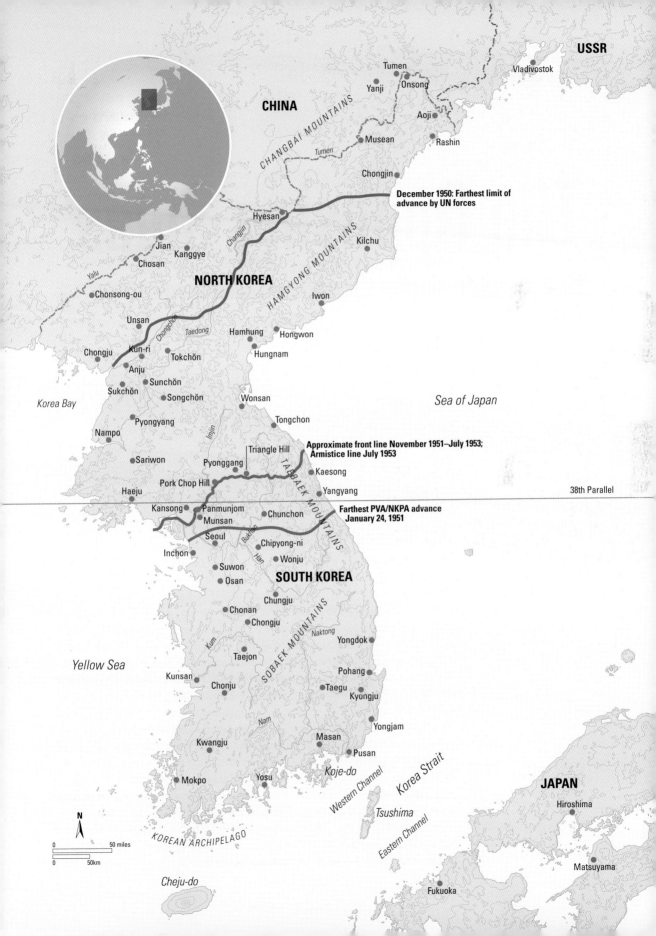

The Opposing Sides

TRAINING

United States

Despite its truly leading role in the defeat of Nazi Germany and imperialist Japan in World War II, the US Army in 1950 was actually ill-prepared to fight a subsequent war in Southeast Asia. As with most post-1945 combatants, the United States embarked on a vast program of demobilization and decommissioning. Some 91 US Army divisions had been formed between 1939 and 1945; by 1950 the US Army consisted of just ten divisions, all understrength. The low readiness for conflict became painfully apparent in the first months of the Korean War. The US Eighth Army, for example, was so short of soldiers in its divisions that it was compelled to implement the Korean Augmentation to the US Army (KATUSA) program, giving 8,300 Republic of Korea (ROK) soldiers five days of conversion training at a training center near Pusan before sending them to pad out US Army divisions. Even with this augmentation, the understrength US Army units initially sent to Korea from occupation duties in Japan were mentally, tactically, and logistically unready for combat. The fact was that between 1945 and 1950, a peacetime mentality had naturally set in.

Training for soldiers in both the Continental United States (CONUS), and for occupation duties in Europe and Japan, was much changed from the wartime years. The US Army cut the basic training program to just eight weeks, down from 14 weeks under wartime conditions. Advanced training now became the responsibility of the unit commander, which meant in reality that in many cases it was simply neglected. Some corrective came in late 1948, following the introduction of the Selective Service Act (also known as the Elston Act) the previous June, which set the groundwork for new wave of conscription. Recognizing that eight

In profound contrast to the light kit and equipment of the PVA soldier, this recruit at Camp Polk, Louisiana, in 1951 has impressive levels of provision. Among the items are his .30-caliber M1 Garand rifle, a bayonet, combat pack, summer and winter uniforms, and sleeping bag. (Munroe/United States Department of State/PhotoQuest/Getty Images)

weeks was not long enough to convert a civilian into a convincing soldier, the Office of the Chief, Army Field Forces (OCAFF) pushed for, and received, an increase in basic training time to 13 weeks, then to 14 weeks in February 1949; but the increase was more focused on developing peacetime soldiering skills rather than improving combat capability. At least half of the training cycle was dedicated to garrison and administrative work (Crane 2019: 27–28).

The Korean War had a transformative effect on US Army military training, in terms of both volume and quality. Eight more training divisions were created during the war (adding to the four already in existence) as were ten Replacement Training Centers. The weight of basic training shifted heavily toward classic infantry combat, concentrating particularly on physical fitness, land navigation, camouflage, cover and concealment, unit tactics, small-arms handling, military communications, infantry–artillery coordination, and other small-unit essentials. The extent of this shift can be gauged by noting that in 1949 garrison duties training occupied 53 percent of the basic training program, but by 1954, the year after the end of Korean hostilities, that figure

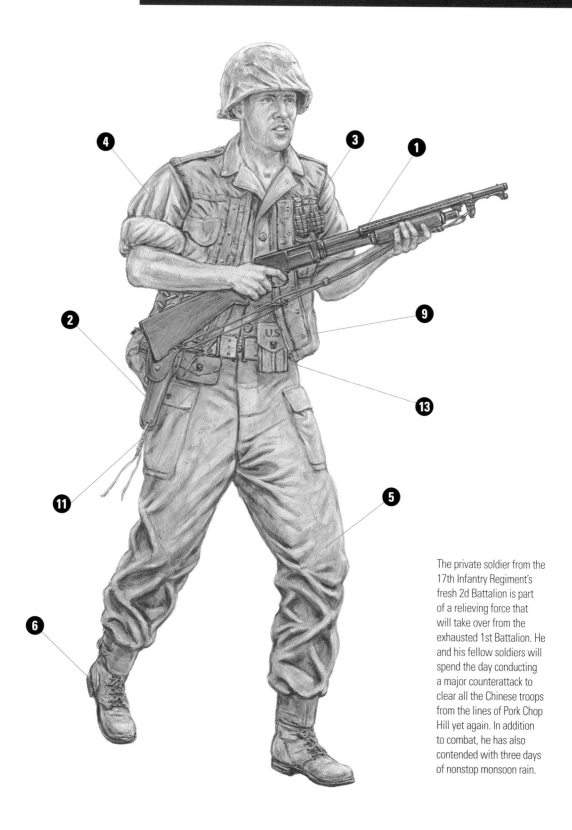

COMBAT

The private soldier from the 17th Infantry Regiment's fresh 2d Battalion is part of a relieving force that will take over from the exhausted 1st Battalion. He and his fellow soldiers will spend the day conducting a major counterattack to clear all the Chinese troops from the lines of Pork Chop Hill yet again. In addition to combat, he has also contended with three days of nonstop monsoon rain.

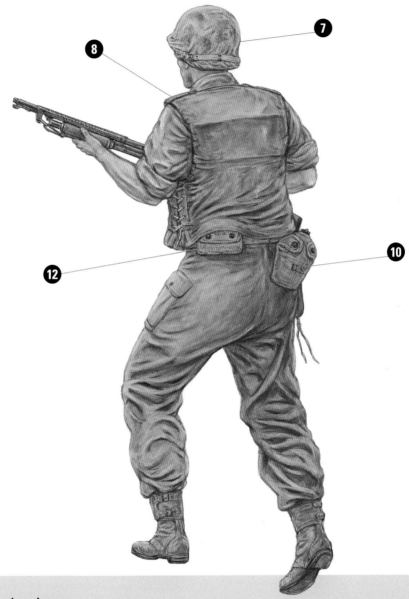

Weapons, dress, and equipment

The soldier is armed with a 12-gauge Stevens 520-30 pump-action trench shotgun (**1**), one of several models, such as the Winchester M97 and M12 pump-action trench shotguns, that had seen service in World War II and which now found a new lease of life in Korea. Such weapons were often assigned to command-post defense missions, but when dealing with a Chinese breakthrough they proved to be extremely effective in cleaning out the PVA assault squads and restoring the perimeters (Swearengen 1978: 215). Despite the weapon's power in short-range combat, it had a limited ammunition capacity and was very slow to reload, so the infantryman also carries a .45-caliber M1911A1 pistol (**2**) as an emergency backup weapon, set in an

M1916 leather holster. He is also armed with two M2 "pineapple" hand grenades (**3**).

Uniform items include an M1943 herringbone twill (HBT) shirt (**4**) with no markings, M1943 HBT trousers (**5**), and M1943 boots (**6**). For head protection the soldier has a standard M1 helmet (**7**) with an improvised cotton cloth cover. He also wears an M1952A ballistic vest (**8**), which had 12 layers of ballistic nylon strong enough to stop shell fragments and some bullets at low velocity, but not high-velocity rounds. His equipment consists of an M1936 belt (**9**), an M1910 canteen in M1941 cover (**10**), an M1924 field dressing pouch (**11**), an M1938 shotgun ammunition pouch (**12**), and a two-cell M1923 .45 caliber pistol magazine pouch (**13**).

August 1950: US troops disembark somewhere in Korea after a long voyage from the United States. The Korean War was no mere sideline for the United States' armed forces; in total, 6.8 million American men and women would serve in the conflict. (Sgt. Dunlap /NARA 111-SC-345283 /Wikimedia/ Public Domain)

had dropped to just 26 percent. During the years of the Korean War, the OCAFF provided basic combat training to 606,447 personnel who had had no previous military experience.

Although the training landscape did improve, the many holes in postwar US defense budgets meant that the quality of training could be patchy. Those soldiers arriving on the front lines for the first time still had to rely upon the experience of senior NCOs and combat-hardened troops to shape them into battle-savvy warriors. The US Army in Korea was also heavily populated by conscripts drafted into the service, with all the variability in morale and motivation that produces. For many US soldiers, Korea was an unknown country fighting an abstract war, and many were both bewildered and scared. This being said, postwar studies of the fighting qualities of US soldiers in the Korean War found that in combat most were every bit as capable as the US soldiers of World War II.

China

The PLA, born out of the protracted revolutionary Chinese Civil War (1927–49), was in 1950 truly vast in terms of manpower compared to the heavily demobilized US Army; it had an astonishing 5.4 million infantry in uniform, making it the largest land army in the world, at least in terms of personnel. Admittedly, the size of the PLA was in part the result of the harsh economic conditions in China at this time; for many men who volunteered for service, the only other option was a life of unrelenting poverty and hardship.

Two influences underwrote the training and ideology of the PLA. First were the principles and practices of revolutionary and guerrilla warfare, encoded by the Chinese leader Mao Zedong and other members of the Chinese military hierarchy. Second was the doctrinal influence and the materiel transfers of the Soviet Union, the personnel and advisors of which became an increasingly prominent presence in China during the Korean War years. When it came to the Korean War itself, the 3 million men and women who served in Korea were technically members of the Chinese People's Volunteer Army (PVA), the name given in an attempt to pretend that it wasn't the Chinese state army fighting the United Nations Command (UNC) forces, although ultimately this adjustment of terminology fooled no one.

At the beginning of the war, PVA soldiers were mostly peasant revolutionaries, led by men who had experience of fighting either the nationalist Chinese or the imperialist Japanese. Training was basic and highly variable, lasting from a few weeks to several months depending on the speed at which replacements were needed on the front line. The training program of the Chinese soldiers who fought in the Korean War roughly broke down into two parts.

First there was an intensive program of political indoctrination, consisting of classroom lectures, confessional activities, propaganda exercises, and a variety of other pursuits, all designed to ensure that the recruit was squarely aligned with communist ideology and Chinese goals. In the context of the Korean War, the political education emphasized threats posed to North Korea's society and family life by the capitalists looming over the border. There might also be basic instruction in reading and writing, as illiteracy was widespread (about 80–85 percent of China's population was illiterate in 1949), a fact that hampered technical combat skills and communications. Then came a generally limited program of combat training, concentrating on small-unit combat tactics and weapons handling, with a particular focus on marksmanship, hand-grenade throwing, bayonet drill, and the use of mines and booby traps. Advanced training was given to machine-gun and mortar teams, so that they could provide the base of fire required for offensive and defensive operations.

Yet for most recruits, more advanced combat instruction began only when they were posted to their operational units and moved into Manchuria prior to deployment in Korea itself. Both in Manchuria and Korea, in-service training concentrated on the specific tactics and terrain they would encounter on the front lines. More time was given to practicing skills such as night assaults, infiltration, coordination with armor and artillery, and the use of mobile automatic firepower. As the war went on, the basic training program was also refined to reflect more closely the tactical realities of the front.

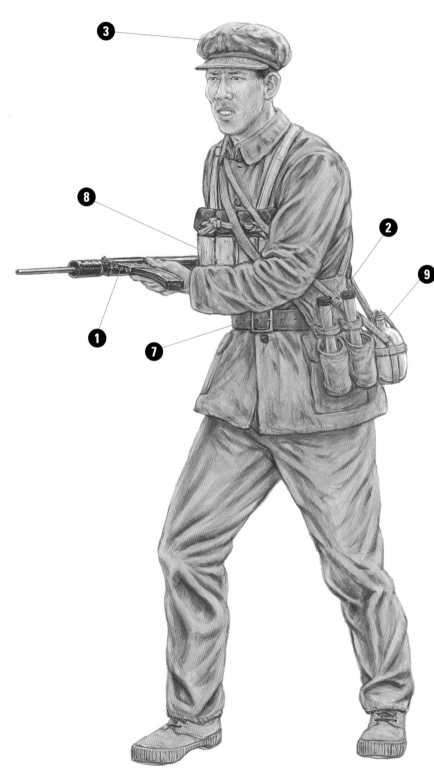

This _Chan-shih_ ("fighter," equivalent to a private) moves down a trench atop Pork Chop Hill on July 8, 1953, on the third day of heavy fighting there. A hardened veteran despite his youth, he wears simple kit and equipment, but needs little else for the close-quarters fighting apart from grenades, ammunition, and water. Here his submachine gun is readied for firing from the hip, the quickest and most instinctive way to fire as he rounds each angle of a trench or enters an enemy-occupied dugout.

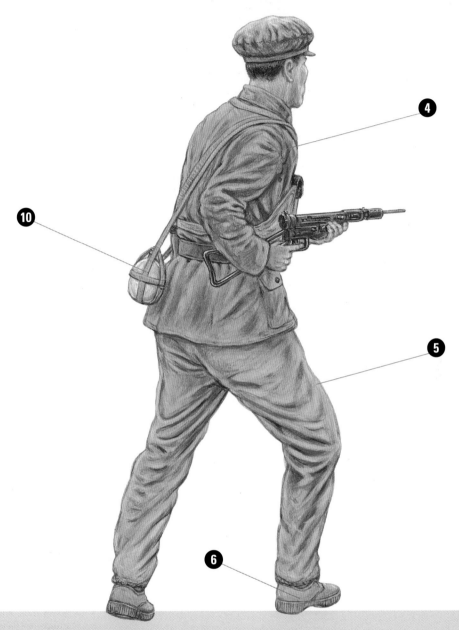

Weapons, dress, and equipment

This soldier carries an M38 submachine gun (**1**), a Chinese-made version of the British 9mm Sten Mk II. During World War II, Canada provided almost 73,000 Sten Mk IIs to Chinese nationalist forces as part of the Mutual Aid Program, but with the collapse of the nationalist cause many of those weapons fell into the hands of the PVA. Some were retained in their original 9mm configuration, but many were adapted to chamber the 7.62×25mm Tokarev cartridge, as in the example shown here. Sten Mk IIs using the Tokarev cartridge had longer barrels (10.5in as opposed to the original 7.7in) and had their magazine wells adapted to take PPS-43 35-round box

magazines. The Chinese not only adapted their stock of Canadian-supplied Sten Mk IIs, but also manufactured their own domestically produced version known as the M38 (in both 9mm and 7.62mm), though these Chinese-made versions dispensed with the select-fire option of the Canadian originals, being fully automatic only. In addition to his firearm, he is armed with a pair of stick grenades (**2**).

His uniform is in the classically simple communist style: a "Mao"-style cap (**3**), a summer tunic (**4**) and trousers (**5**), and canvas shoes (**6**) with rubber soles. He is equipped with a belt (**7**), M38 submachine gun ammunition pouches (**8**), a grenade harness (**9**), and a water bottle (**10**).

Riding in a US Jeep, Chairman Mao reviews his army in late 1949 or early 1950. The weapons in the background appear to be 37mm M1939 antiaircraft autocannon, a Soviet weapon the Chinese later copied as the Type 55. (Universal History Archive/ UIG via Getty Images)

The training programs were not helped by the patchwork of weapon systems within the PVA (see below). This situation complicated small-unit combat training and battlefield logistics; indeed for some PVA soldiers the first time they fired live ammunition was in action. Yet this did not prevent the Chinese forces in Korea as a whole from operating with tactical intelligence and high levels of morale and motivation.

As the Korean War progressed, the PVA received increasing volumes of foreign weaponry, largely from the Soviet Union, instruction in which was facilitated by 3,642 Soviet advisors who worked in China and the Korean theater between 1950 and 1953. As a result, Chinese infantry training became a little more sophisticated in all-arms combat, particularly synchronization between infantry assaults and artillery barrages. In pure military terms, the Chinese soldier remained unsophisticated compared to his US Army equivalent across the lines, but with a basic set of weapons and equipment he could still achieve formidable results.

Civilians sign up to join the PVA, eager to commit themselves to their national duty in the war in Korea. To encourage greater volumes of recruits, a national Volunteer Movement Committee was formed in 1950 by the PLA and the Chinese Communist Party (CCP). (USAG-Humphreys/Flickr/CC BY 2.0)

WEAPONS

United States

The weapons of the US Army infantry in the Korean War were essentially those it had taken into battle during World War II, with some focused improvements and redistributions among the squads, platoons, and companies. The trusty mainstay of the US Army rifleman was the .30-06 M1 Garand, an eight-shot semiautomatic rifle. Although internationally the M1 was starting to show its age by the time of the Korean War, as the Soviets introduced the 7.62mm AK-47 assault rifle, it was superior to many of the bolt-action rifles fielded by other forces in the theater and its reliability and punch were still appreciated by the US Army's infantryman. Lighter, more portable firepower came in the form of the .30-caliber M2 Carbine, a select-fire version of the M1 Carbine that had seen extensive use in World War II. The M2 was a gas-operated weapon firing from a 15- or 30-round detachable box magazine, with a full-auto option at a cyclical rate of 750rd/min. Although the US Army platoon Tables of Organization and Equipment (TO&E) had limited issue of the M2, principally to automatic weapon ammunition bearers, its battlefield distribution was wider, as troops appreciated its close-quarters firepower, superior accuracy compared to the older generations of submachine guns, and comfortable portability. Therefore it was not uncommon to see the M2 Carbine in the hands of platoon commanders and senior NCOs, as well as those of many other troops. The days of the submachine gun were not done, however – the .45-caliber M3/M3A1 "Grease Gun" was also in widespread use, and numbers of .45-caliber M1A1 Thompsons were also to be seen. Most officers and some enlisted men also carried the standard US Army .45-caliber M1911A1 semiautomatic pistol as a backup weapon; officers might also be armed with a variety of .38-caliber revolvers.

Automatic support fire at platoon level was provided by one, later two, .30-caliber M1918A2 Browning Automatic rifles (BARs) in each rifle squad. Although the BAR was a redoubtable and powerful weapon, its 20-round detachable box magazine feed and fixed barrel meant its suppression capabilities were limited. For more sustained fire, the US Army drew on the .30-caliber Browning M1919A6, a belt-fed light machine gun that could be both bipod- and tripod-mounted; one, later two, of these weapons were operated in the rifle-platoon weapon squad. There were also

the .50-caliber Browning M2 heavy machine guns held in the battalion weapons company, which could deploy four M2s and four M1919A6s. For the ultimate in heavy automatic firepower, however, the divisional Antiaircraft Artillery Automatic Weapon (AAA AW) battalion could deploy its M45 Quadmount – four M2HB (heavy barrel) heavy machine guns configured in pairs on one mount – and 40mm antiaircraft (AA) weapons in the ground-support role; with the barrels leveled horizontal, these weapons could deliver the most destructive firepower imaginable, and were much feared by the Chinese.

Also in the squad or the platoon headquarters was a shoulder-launched "bazooka" rocket launcher, mainly used in Korea for "bunker busting." At first, the US forces in Korea went into action with the World War II-era 2.36in M9A1 antitank rocket launcher, but when this proved largely incapable of destroying North Korean People's Army (NKPA) T-34-85 medium tanks it was replaced by the more potent 3.5in M20 "Super Bazooka," which could penetrate up to 11in of armor – more than double the capability of the M9A1. The heavy-weapons company also featured a recoilless rifle platoon, the weapons of which had similar purposes to the bazookas but packed greater punch and range. The smallest type was the 57mm M18 recoilless rifle, a light shoulder- or tripod-mounted weapon with an effective range of about 490yd; three of these weapons were issued

US troops fighting in Seoul in September 1950. Two men are armed with .30-caliber M2 Carbines, fitted with the standard 15-round magazine. Analysis of the combat performance of the M2 found that ammunition depletion was a problem when inexperienced soldiers switched to full-auto fire; more savvy troops tended to keep their M2 on semi-auto fire and focus more on individual shot accuracy. (Lt. Strickland/Cpl. Romanowski/defenseimagery.mil/Wikimedia/Public Domain)

to each rifle company. They struggled to make an impression on tanks, however, so were mainly used against hardened defensive positions. For genuine antiarmor capability, the infantry could use the heavier 75mm M20 and 105mm M27 recoilless rifles. The former, mounted on either a .30-caliber machine-gun tripod or a light vehicle, was particularly useful, with its effective range (with high-explosive shells) of more than 1,000yd and a penetration with high-explosive antitank (HEAT) shells of 3.9in of rolled homogenous armor. The penetration figure meant the M20 could still struggle to defeat a T-34, however. The M27 was theoretically a far better tank-killer, but it was rushed into production and was inaccurate (it featured no integral spotting rifle), awkwardly heavy, and unreliable.

Most of the infantry mortars were operated by the mortar platoon within the heavy-weapons company. Five main types of mortar were used by the US forces in the Korean War: 60mm M2 and M19, 81mm M1, 4.2in M2, and 107mm M30. Mortars proved their utility in the Korean War, their high arcs of fire making them ideal for use from emplaced and protected positions, including those on the reverse sides of slopes. They were more mobile and quicker to bring into action than heavy field artillery and their high rates of fire (an 81mm M1, for example, had a flat-out emergency rate of fire of up to 35rd/min) meant that they were invaluable for countering massed Chinese troops heading toward the wire.

China

While the US forces had a prescribed body of weapons according to set TO&E, the Chinese, by contrast, fielded a bewildering variety of weapons drawn from a diverse variety of sources, the "pick-and-mix" approach being essential to equip a nascent multi-million-man army. In addition to license-built weapons or unlicensed copies manufactured indigenously, such as the

This very grainy image shows PVA troops in defiant mood. All are armed with either the Soviet 7.62mm PPSh-41 *Papasha* ("Daddy") submachine gun or the Chinese Type 50, a licensed copy. Submachine guns were ideal for PVA infantry tactics – the PPSh-41/Type 50 had a cyclical rate of fire of more than 1,000rd/min, which had a devastating effect in close-quarters assaults on US Army-held trenches and bunkers. (Unknown/ Wikimedia/Public Domain)

7.92mm Type 24 (Gewehr 98) and 7.92mm Hanyang 88 (Gewehr 88) bolt-action rifles, the 7.62mm Type 49 and Type 50 (PPSh-41) submachine guns, and the 57mm Type 36 (M18) recoilless rifle, the PVA was equipped with tens of thousands of weapons captured from the Chinese nationalists (many of which had been supplied by the United States), the Imperial Japanese Army, and from UNC and ROK forces, to which can be added Soviet acquisitions and some European types. Thus a PVA infantry unit might be armed with Japanese 7.7mm Arisaka, German 7.92mm Mauser, and Soviet 7.62mm Mosin-Nagant rifles; German 9mm MP 40, US .45 ACP Thompson, and Chinese 7.62mm Type 50 submachine guns; and Soviet 7.62mm Degtyaryov DP-27, Japanese 7.9mm Type 99, and Czech 7.92mm ZB-26 light machine guns, among many others. Similar variety could be found among the heavier support weapons as well. A US Marine Corps report of Chinese weapons captured following a battle was representative: "Ironically enough it was with US weapons that the Chinese were for the most part armed. These included 60 and 81 mm mortars, Thompson sub-machine guns, and heavy and light machine guns, most of which had been captured from Chinese Nationalist forces" (1st Marine Division 1950: 29–30).

The PVA placed a particularly heavy emphasis on the use of grenades, which its infantry would throw in significant volumes during both offensive and defensive operations. The most common of these was the Type 67, a variant copy of the German M24 *Stielhandgranate* ("stick grenade"), but the PVA also hurled several types of Soviet fragmentation grenade. It was also a prolific user of the Bangalore torpedo, which along with demolition

This group of Chinese soldiers, captured south of Koto-ri in late 1950, give a good impression of PVA winter clothing. Note the variety of footwear: fur-lined winter boots were available to some, but many soldiers retained lightweight civilian-type shoes and sneakers. (Sgt. F.C. Kerr (USMC)/Wikimedia/Public Domain)

Soldiers of the PVA march south into the Korean war zone. Although China received increasing numbers of military trucks from the Soviet Union as the war progressed, long-distance foot marches remained the primary method of troop deployment for the PVA during the conflict. (USAG-Humphreys/Flickr/ CC BY 2.0)

satchel charges was useful for clearing perimeter defenses or for assaulting trench lines.

The miscellany of Chinese weapons certainly did not make for streamlined inventories. The PVA did rationalize its units as much as it could; for example, we sometimes find that PVA assault units were all equipped with PPSh-41-type submachine guns, although given that much of our photographic record of the Chinese forces was taken for propaganda purposes, such evidence needs to be treated with some caution. The fact remained that the PVA was, to a large extent, an army of small-unit weaponry, the vast majority of soldiers going into battle with a personal weapon, about 80 rounds of ammunition, four or five grenades, and possibly some satchel charges and mortar bombs (for the nearby mortar team). Given some reasonable artillery support, these basically equipped soldiers were more than capable of prosecuting highly effective battles.

TACTICS

The tactics of the Korean War can largely be broken down into the mobile warfare period between June 1950 and mid-1951 and the fighting across largely static front lines between 1951 and war's end in June 1953. Here we will assess the overarching tactical patterns as laid down by doctrine and experience, a picture then refined in the "Analysis" chapter below using the specific examples of the battles for Chipyong-ni, Triangle Hill, and Pork Chop Hill.

United States

The tactical framework employed by the US Army during the Korean War was a mixture of World War II experience, immediate post-1945 revisions to wartime doctrines, and combat innovations prompted by experience in Korea itself. Regarding offensive tactics, doctrine essentially laid down classic principles of maneuver warfare. Frontal attack in the age of modern firepower was rarely recommended, but in small actions in difficult terrain it might often be the only choice available to the attacker. Keys to the successful frontal attack were surprise, speed of advance, and heavy suppressive fire from artillery and other support weapons. Far more preferable, however, was "envelopment," in which the main attacking force would drive into and around the enemy flank, while a supporting frontal attack both distracted the enemy from the flank attack and "fixed" him in place, limiting his possibilities for counter-maneuvers. "Penetration," by contrast, involved a concentrated main attack against a weak point in the enemy line, assisted by adjacent supporting attacks; the aim was for the main attack to punch through the enemy line, thereby creating new flanks that could be turned. With the "turning movement," one force would be deployed deep behind enemy positions to cut his lines of communication, while a frontal attacking force sought to breach defenses from the front, creating the classic "hammer-and-anvil" grip on the enemy, trapped between two forces. This approach was especially suited to US airborne forces, which could be dropped into the "anvil" position en masse, courtesy of US superiority in air power and vertical envelopment.

All the conventional offensive infantry tactics had their place in the fighting in Korea, but there had to be many conflict-specific adaptations. The difficult Korean terrain, for example, often dictated the physical limits of unit

A soldier of the US Army's 2d Infantry Division mans a .30-caliber Browning M1917A1 machine gun near Yeongsan, South Korea. The M1917A1 was showing its age by the time of the Korean War, although its water-cooled system enabled it to deliver better sustained fire than the air-cooled Brownings. (USAG-Humphreys/Flickr/CC BY 2.0)

size, unit formation (e.g. column instead of line), and routes of advance in the attack, with the result that during the War of the Outposts, in particular, US frontal attacks were frequently the only tactical option; there might be no flanks to turn and no weak points to penetrate in a 360-degree perimeter defense atop a mountain. Also, at first the US forces in Korea tended to move through valleys without securing the high ground either side – a prime invitation for enemy ambush and attrition from the heights above. Hard lessons were learned: from 1951 any movement through a valley was accompanied by security units taking the high ground both sides of the lower advance. Another tactical lesson learned by US forces was to halt pursuing attacks during the nighttime hours, despite all the advantages the Americans brought in terms of illumination technologies. It soon became clear that the Chinese were particularly adept at digging-in quickly as the light faded from the day, even as the US soldiers struggled to negotiate darkened and shadowy terrain. It was simply too costly to prosecute the attack under these circumstances.

When it came to defense, the tactics laid down in FM 100-5, *Field Service Regulations, Operations*, were fairly standard for the period. The focus was on establishing a defense in depth. The principal defensive artery was the main line of resistance (MLR), a network of defenses consisting of fortified and entrenched weapon positions, heavy concentrations of both direct and indirect firepower (including artillery and mortars), interlocking fields of fire, and obstacles such as barbed wire and minefields to channel the enemy into predesignated kill zones. Out in front of the MLR were the combat outpost line, consisting of forward positions acting in support of specific battalions, and the general outpost line stretching intermittently across the whole front. The purpose of these forward forces was to inflict delay, casualties, disruption, and confusion upon the enemy before he even reached the MLR. The theory was that the moment the enemy came into contact with US forces, he would be subjected to a grinding attrition that rendered him combat ineffective by the time he reached the MLR. The defense would also have a mobile reserve farther back to draw into action should parts of the MLR be threatened with penetration, and to exploit counterattack opportunities.

US experience in Korea compelled a series of innovations in defensive tactics, some born out of desperation. In Korea, the US Army often did not have enough troops to create unbroken lines of defense stretching across miles of undulating landscape. Instead, the US Army came to rely more on a "mobile defense" approach, in which much of the defensive strength was held back in the mobile reserve, to be unleashed once forward outposts identified the direction and strength of the enemy onslaught.

The Eighth United States Army in Korea (EUSAK), particularly under the leadership of Lieutenant General (later General) Matthew B. Ridgway, who took over command after the death of Lieutenant General Walton H. Walker in a traffic accident on December 23, 1950, also brought in new perspectives on the establishment of defensive positions in complex and mountainous terrain. Ridgway stipulated that in the absence of a continuous defensive line, units should at night occupy elevated positions, such as hilltops and ridge lines, which offered all-around defensive qualities. Thus

they could not only establish a defensible perimeter, but with the benefits of elevation they could also observe and note enemy movements through valleys. Having good observation posts also meant better communications and coordination with artillery, close air support (CAS), and the mobile reserve. Such defensive positions, however, had little in the way of depth, instead being relatively shallow chains strung across the terrain, with fire support coming only from adjacent units.

The US Army's defenses were tested to the extreme by Chinese mass attacks and infiltration tactics (see below). Recognizing that defensive positions might be occupied for significant lengths of time against heavy assaults, front-line units made greater investments in creating more "hardened" fighting positions, with more resilient levels of cover and improved concealment of foxholes, trenches, and bunkers, and more complex interconnections between positions to obstruct the enemy if he managed to enter the complex. The volumes of available firepower were increased, especially the density of machine guns (the M45 "Quad Fifty" machine-gun unit was particularly popular in the ground-fire role), recoilless rifles, bazookas, mortars, and flamethrowers. Mines and booby traps, tripwire flares, napalm-type "fougasse" explosives (see below), barbed wire, preregistered artillery, and other grim ingenuities made the offensive approaches to US defensive positions particularly costly for the attacker. At night, US Army units would often also use powerful searchlights to illuminate the ground for miles around them, although this measure was a double-edged sword, as the searchlights could also provide the illumination that enabled Chinese forces to maneuver more effectively in the dark.

A US Army mortar crew lay down fire from their 4.2in M2 heavy mortar in Korea in 1953. The mortar is emplaced in a well-constructed firing position typical of the later years of the Korean War, the position having substantial layers of protective sandbags and a separate bunker for ammunition storage and personal cover. (Sgt. Guy A. Kassal/PD-USGOV-MILITARY-ARMY/Wikimedia/Public Domain)

US soldiers in Korea fire a 75mm M20 recoilless rifle. As is evident here, the backblast of the M20 was substantial. It was imperative that no troops were standing immediately behind the weapon when it was fired, while the kick-up of dust could provide a visual indicator of the weapon's position to enemy gunners. (US Army/Wikimedia/Public Domain)

Firepower was undoubtedly the US Army infantryman's friend in the Korean War, and he usually had plenty of it upon which to draw, especially in the forms of tube artillery and CAS from ground-attack aircraft. For front-line infantry units thunderous support fire frequently made the difference between victory and defeat or between survival and destruction in the face of massed Chinese attacks. Problems in accessing or coordinating such fire, however, were common in the more mountainous areas, where the terrain and topography interfered with radio communications or with the long arcs of artillery shells. Infantry units might also enjoy the reassuring support of armor. In the absence of adequate tube artillery, sometimes tanks would park themselves on reverse slopes facing upward, the gradient of the slope increasing the elevation of the main gun, allowing it to serve as improvisatory field artillery.

One Korean War US defensive tactical innovation of note was developed by I Corps in 1951, and became known as "fight and roll." It was especially applicable to coping with unrelenting waves of Chinese attacks. The tactic involved the defenders holding onto their positions as long as possible, inflicting the maximum attrition upon the enemy in the process. Just at the point when they were about to be overwhelmed, the defenders would pull out quickly to prepared defensive positions farther back. This process would

A US soldier makes a report via field telephone from a trench system. The undulating topography of Korea was challenging for both wired and wireless communications, with incessant ridges, hills, summits, and rivers interfering with radio signals and the laying of wired communications. Typically, a position headquarters had a wired telephone to higher headquarters, with VHF wireless as a backup. (Keystone/Getty Images)

be repeated, sometimes as many as five or six times, as the enemy attack surged onward. With each successive stage, the energy would steadily bleed out of the enemy offensive. As described by a I Corps report: "[Enemy] Units will be decimated, command and control channels lost and equipment gone. The mass becomes a struggling, chaotic mixture of the remnants of many broken units" (quoted in Doughty 1979: 10). Once the enemy was dropping to his knees, then the US forces would launch reserve troops forward in a counterattack, hopefully to retake the initiative.

China

The popular image of Chinese tactics in the Korean War is of a broiling mass of undifferentiated manpower being thrown against US positions in crude, costly, but terrifying "human wave" frontal assaults, a sea of bodies fed into the mouths of US guns. There is an element of truth to this. In the early years of the Korean War, Maoist military philosophy favored manpower over firepower when it came to infantry tactics. It was also ideologically governed by the principles of revolutionary war, with its strong focus on wearing down the enemy relentlessly over time, whatever the cost: "the enemy advances, we retreat; the enemy camps, we harass; the enemy tires, we attack; the enemy retreats, we pursue," was a classic codification of guerrilla warfare.

Yet there was both logic and method behind PVA tactics. Certainly, the Chinese forces did not have the technological, logistical, or organizational sophistication of the US and (most) UN forces, but they compensated for their weaknesses admirably, and were an exceptionally tough and respected enemy for even the best of US troops.

Chinese offensive tactics drew on the recognition that the US and UN forces were often spread thinly across the front, with weak points there to be exploited. The PVA was particularly adept at covert nighttime reconnaissance and infiltration, identifying gaps and vulnerabilities in the enemy lines with unnerving precision. Conventionally, this assessment was achieved with patrols and keen-eyed observers, but sometimes more unorthodox approaches bore fruit. For example, PVA troops might blow bugles and flutes as if an attack was to being launched, provoking an outburst of US firepower that actually served to identify firing positions. PVA intelligence operatives might attempt to penetrate the enemy lines while pretending to be South Korean civilians, although this became a harder ploy to pull off once the fighting became largely static.

The key focus of Chinese offensive tactics was either to envelop or encircle the enemy position or to penetrate it at the weak points. If prior detailed reconnaissance had not been possible, one PVA approach tactic was to have two units deployed forward with one following behind. When the formation ran up against the US defenses, one of the forward units was pulled back and the one that remained forward made a series of probing attacks, repeatedly trying to find points of exploitation. Once those were identified, elements of the two units farther back were sent forward to make a concentrated effort at penetration. The goal was to drive through the enemy front line, after which advance forces would engage the inevitable counterattack from the US reserves, while the units to the rear would attempt to encircle the defenders' MLR. A similar attack tactic to this "one up, two back" approach was developed by Chinese forces operating in Korea. It was essentially a Chinese form of encirclement, with two units performing a simultaneous assault on both flanks of the enemy position while a heavy-weapons unit concentrated fire to the front.

The PVA, as noted above, certainly did employ human-wave attacks, although rather than seeing them as crude charges we should regard them as purposeful efforts to find weak points and overwhelm the enemy defenses. There was organization within the mass. Frequently, the PVA would attack at night, driving the spearhead companies as close as possible, sometimes to within 20yd of the front lines, before opening up with their weapons. The priority for the first waves of attackers would be to destroy key machine-gun, mortar, recoilless rifle, and other support weapon positions, these men relying heavily on grenades, demolitions, and light-machine-gun suppression. Often each three-man squad would be given a specific position to assault. Subsequent waves would thereafter attempt to penetrate trench and bunker systems, and negate US firepower advantages in close-quarters combat.

We must also acknowledge that command-and-control in Chinese units was extremely basic. There were almost no radios in use below regimental level, thus at battalion level and below battlefield communications were

enforced by a mixture of audible and visual means – bugles, horns, whistles, and flares (Keegan 1981: 48). With this in mind, battlefield tactics had to be simple and repetitive to work, in much the same way that British soldiers walked across the battlefields of the Western Front in World War I to ensure unit cohesion in the absence of real-time communications. In the Korean War the repeated attacks spilled Chinese blood by the gallon, but the intrinsic discipline of the assaults, inculcated through unrelenting drills and ideological motivation, meant that if the US/UNC forces weakened at any point, the Chinese forces would seize the moment and surge through.

The PVA forces took to heart the lesson the Soviet forces had learned during World War II: when faced by an enemy with superior firepower, they sought to "hug" him close to neutralize the advantage. During the static phases of the Korean War in 1951–53, therefore, the gap between US and Chinese lines could be unnervingly short. Furthermore, the Chinese proved highly adept in fieldcraft, particularly the skills of finding and making cover, camouflage, and concealment. In short, Chinese soldiers were elusive figures to spot in the terrain, and they used such skills to perform the most audacious and repeated infiltrations. Small infiltration units would approach US positions silently under cover of darkness, then open up at very close range with automatic weapons while hurling copious numbers of grenades as a form of personal artillery barrage. (Chinese infantry training placed particular emphasis on the skills of grenade handling.)

Chinese soldiers of the 39th Division conduct an assault in the Wonsan area in November 1950. Because of a general lack of small-unit wireless communications, individual soldiers needed to stay close to their squad leader to adhere to the battle plan. (USAG-Humphreys/Flickr/CC BY 2.0)

This rare photograph shows PVA troops conducting an assault in early 1951. A mortar team, armed with a 60mm Type 31 light mortar (a Chinese copy of the US M2), lay down suppressive fire while members of an infantry squad rush quickly into the attack, trying to gain their objectives before US firepower can be brought to bear. (USAG-Humphreys/Flickr/CC BY 2.0)

Defensively, the PVA repurposed the "one up, two back" approach outlined above. This tactic involved having one unit as a strong covering force, its purpose being to act as a protective screen that could delay an enemy counterattack once it came. The two units farther back provided a mobile response, pushing forward to strengthen the line where it was most threatened or to counterattack if possible.

The PVA's primitive logistical arrangements were potentially its greatest weakness, but in many ways they actually became an operational strength. The lack of vehicular logistics – during the initial offensive in late 1950 the Chinese had just 300 trucks to support 300,000 soldiers – meant individual soldiers tended to be impressively physically fit, capable of marching fast over long distances or scrambling relentlessly up steep terrain. One Chinese force, for example, covered 286 miles of mountain elevations and ridges in just 19 days. A US infantry division required approximately 385 tons of supplies per day to function; but a Chinese division needed just 44 tons. Each PVA soldier would typically carry about five days of emergency rations (rice, tea, salt) on his person, but the bulk of the logistics was hauled by peasant porters operating at night, each porter carrying about 80–100lb via a shoulder-mounted bamboo pole with a basket on each end. The foot-mounted logistics might have been crude, but they were also ideally suited to operations in difficult terrain, and gave the Chinese impressive tactical

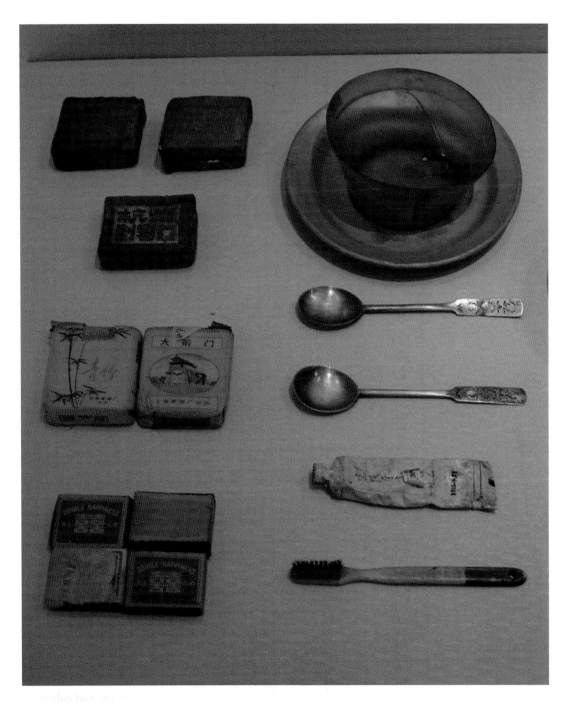

mobility. Without a long and heavy logistical train, the PVA could also maintain a relentless tempo of movement and maneuver to keep the enemy on the back foot.

Whether on the attack or the defense, the PVA was a respected enemy of the US Army. It was adaptable, extremely aggressive, and generally good with the weapons it had. As a US Marine Corps report noted in late 1950 after a major Chinese attack: "The attacking troops were well armed, well trained, well-equipped, and ably led" (US Marine Corps 1950: 29–30).

This photograph, taken from an exhibition at the War Memorial of Korea in Seoul, South Korea, shows the minimal personal effects carried by a typical PVA soldier. The advantage of light personal logistics was an ability to move quickly and easily. (Tksteven/Wikimedia/ CC BY-SA 2.5)

Chipyong-ni

February 5–15, 1951

BACKGROUND TO BATTLE

Fought between February 13 and 15, 1951, the battle of Chipyong-ni is a perfect example of a little-known engagement with a high status among students of military tactics. Those three violent days pitted a reinforced US regimental combat team (RCT) against several divisions' worth of PVA forces, in the process offering up a near-textbook model of an intelligent and gutsy all-around defense. Such was the importance of this unequal struggle in the overall war that it has been referred to as "the Gettysburg of the Korean War."

For a time in late 1950, it seemed entirely realistic to contemplate a UN, and a US, defeat in Korea. The Chinese invasion had rewritten the nature and rules of the conflict. The initial PVA offensive was effected by some 300,000 men led by Peng Dehuai, a veteran Chinese commander with immense combat experience and a strong intuitive sense of the battlefield. His principal instruments were the PVA's IX and XIII Army groups, the latter containing a very high ratio of combat-seasoned professionals spread across four armies, while the three armies of IX Army Group consisted primarily of new recruits, whose main experience was training for an invasion of Taiwan. (Note that in Chinese terminology the term 'army group' is more equivalent to a western "army" and the term "army" is more equivalent to "corps.") Unfortunately for the US forces at Chipyong-ni, it would be the men of XIII Army Group against whom they would be pitted.

By the time the Chinese participation in the Korean War began in October 1950, the US and UN leadership had resolutely ignored weeks of warning signs. The forces of the UNC had pushed farther and farther north, flush with overconfidence. In the process, its lines of advance became more attenuated and vulnerable. Confidence that the Chinese would stay out of the war ran to

the highest levels of command: MacArthur himself reassured President Harry S. Truman that the Chinese would, despite their protestations, remain on their side of the border. Peng, meanwhile, spotted the opportunity to draw the UNC into a trap. On October 14, 1950, he committed XIII Army Group across the Yalu River, in what was known as the "First Wave Offensive." This unexpected surge of Chinese communist troops inflicted a sharp defeat on the ROK II Corps, but the Chinese then settled into positions and waited expectantly. As Peng intended, many in the UNC believed that the Chinese were making a limited and geographically shallow intervention. EUSAK and the US X Corps resumed the advance once again in November, stretching the UNC's already thin logistics lines even further.

With the UNC forces heading north, Peng eventually sprang the trap in his "Second Phase Offensive." Both of his army groups were now committed in full, the Chinese aim being to obliterate or encircle the ROK II Corps and the US I and IX corps, inflicting a decisive defeat. Chaos ensued within the UNC, as an entire coalition army attempted to evade destruction. Sustained Chinese attacks, conducted at a relentlessly high tempo, threw the US forces into disarray and retreat, with heavy casualties incurred. The US troops turned and headed southward at speed through a freezing winter landscape, their lines of retreat often harried by Chinese attacks on both flanks. The retreat took the UNC forces all the way back to and across the 38th Parallel, undoing almost all the gains made since the Inchon landings of mid-September 1950. (The unfortunate city of Seoul would change hands four times during the war, with repetitively catastrophic consequences for its beleaguered civilian population.) Panic extended to the top brass; MacArthur himself argued to Truman that the UNC faced outright defeat if the United States did not immediately widen its war effort to include mainland China. The prospect of using atomic weapons to counter the Chinese threat hung in the air.

The PVA was actually riding on the crest of a weakening wave. It had put the UNC forces into retreat with significant casualties, but what it had not achieved was the decisive encirclement and destruction of the major UNC formations. The US 2d Infantry Division, for example, had managed to

A US Army M46 Patton medium tank lays down fire in support of infantry operations, Korea, 1952. The utility of armor was limited during the static phase of warfare in Korea between 1951 and 1953, but tanks could still be useful as a form of protected direct-fire artillery, as witnessed at Chipyong-ni. (NARA/Wikimedia/Public Domain)

break out down the Kunu-ri–Sunchon road in late November 1950, despite taking approximately 5,000 casualties and losing most of its vehicles and heavy weapons in the process. Also in late November 1950, the 1st Marine Division, in an action still spoken of with reverence to this day, conducted an epic fighting breakout from around the Chosin Reservoir, hammering out aggressive counterattacks even as it pulled back south, punishing the Chinese forces heavily every time they made an assault. Across the front, by the time the UNC forces had reached the 38th Parallel the PVA had suffered 20,000 dead, many of them falling victim to US artillery and air support to which the Chinese had little effective answer. As 1950 gave way to 1951 it was clear that China was not holding all the cards.

Truman and the other UN political leaders adamantly resisted widening the war, rightly fearing the possibility of a superpower conflict with the Soviet Union. Instead, the overall war goals were significantly reduced in a strategic directive of December 29, 1950. In this act, the reunification of Korea under the ROK was abandoned, the focus being instead on stopping China's expansionism and preserving the ROK's existing territory. The UNC forces retreated to a line running (east–west) Samcheok–Wonju–Suwon and dug in. The change of command of EUSAK in late December would have a restorative effect on US morale and tactical initiative. Ridgway sought to change EUSAK's mindset from defeatism to offensive aggression. He advocated a new "meatgrinder" approach to the Chinese, using US firepower to inflict the heaviest possible casualties on the enemy while giving up as little ground as possible. Although Peng's "Third Phase Offensive," launched on December 31, 1950, retook Seoul for the communists, it soon after ran out of steam with terrible numbers of casualties.

Then came the US pushback. In January 1951 Ridgway launched two major reconnaissance-in-force operations, *Wolfhound* and *Thunderbolt*, following which US X Corps (Major General Edward M. Almond) made a major northward advance from February 5 in Operation *Roundup*, to straighten out US X Corps' line with that of the ROK III Corps to its right. The line of departure for the operation was to be in US X Corps' zone of operations, and ran from Chipyong-ni in the west, through Hoengsong, and out to Pyeongchang. The US 2d Infantry Division detached the battle-hardened 23d RCT, commanded by the exceptional Colonel Paul L. Freeman, Jr., to secure Chipyong-ni, which the unit did in a sudden push on February 2–3 without major problems; the Americans observed enemy activity on nearby Hill 506, but no engagement ensued. Startled by the US gains, the PVA then launched its "Fourth Phase Offensive" on February 11, driving south again with an estimated 21 Chinese and nine NKPA divisions. Ridgway pulled back all the UNC forces except the 23d RCT at Chipyong-ni, which would essentially act as a breakwater against the advancing enemy, preventing him from moving freely down the Han River valley.

Chipyong-ni itself was a diminutive battleground – a minor Korean village, but one with a critical road intersection in its midst, the incoming roads snaking between multiple surrounding peaks. The village was thus critical to both the UNC's defense and the PVA's offense. The 23d RCT consisted of three infantry battalions, the 1st Ranger Company, the tough

volunteers of the French Battalion of the United Nations Organization, a combat-engineer company, heavy mortars, a battalion of 105mm howitzers, a battery of 155mm howitzers, a company of 14 tanks, six M16 half-tracks each mounting an M45 Quadmount machine-gun unit, and four 40mm Mk 19 twin cannon. In total, Freeman had 4,500 men, 2,500 of whom were combat infantry.

By the time Freeman moved his command into positions at Chipyong-ni on February 5, the formation had already given the Chinese a beating in the battle of the Twin Tunnels, just to the southeast of Chipyong-ni, on February 1, in which it had effectively destroyed the PVA 125th Division. The Chinese forces massing against Chipyong-ni were now, however, immensely strong in manpower: elements of five divisions, totaling between 6,000 and 10,000 men. Freeman recognized that his salient forward position would quickly be surrounded by such a mass of manpower, and at first he requested permission to pull his formation back and incorporate it into the main US line. This request was refused, so Freeman established a 360-degree perimeter defense, key points of the perimeter being the rail line to the south of the village and the lower slopes (those facing the US troops) of Hills 348 and 506 to the north/northeast. He immediately began making exhaustive, intelligent defensive preparations, ensuring that his troops created optimal fields of fire, defendable positions, rationalized supply dumps, and good intra- and inter-unit communications (see pp.71–74 for more detail). He placed his companies around the perimeter in clockwise fashion: 1st Battalion (Cos A and C only) at the 12 to 1 o'clock position; 3d Battalion (Cos I, L, and K) at 2 to 5 o'clock; 2d Battalion (Cos E, F, and G) at 5 to 7 o'clock; the French Battalion at 7 to 12 o'clock; and Co. B, 1st Battalion, and 1st Ranger Company held in the center as a reserve. As isolated as Freeman's troops were, they were ready to fight.

This US soldier in Korea has a .30-caliber M1 Carbine fitted with an M3 Sniperscope, one of the first generation of active infrared night-vision devices. It was a bulky piece of equipment, with a rubberized canvas carry case holding a 12-volt battery to power the 20,000-volt scope. (A. Lambert/Fairfax Media via Getty Images)

MAP KEY

1 **February 5–12:** The 23d RCT, led by Colonel Freeman, establishes an all-around perimeter defense at Chipyong-ni, extending out from the village into the lower foothills of key terrain features.

2 **February 12:** PVA forces maneuver themselves into position around Chipyong-ni, preparing for a major infantry assault against the US perimeter.

3 **2330hrs, February 13:** After more than an hour of preparatory fires, the Chinese forces launch a full-scale assault on the US perimeter, attacking with multiple waves of infantry.

4 **0100hrs, February 14:** The PVA 359th Regiment attempts to break the northern US defenses by moving across high ground to assault the flank of C/23d Infantry, but the assault is repulsed.

5 **0200hrs, February 14:** Units from the PVA 344th Regiment begin a concentrated effort to cut out G/23d Infantry's section of the perimeter. The fighting, over several hours, sees the Chinese drive the 3d Platoon out of its positions, which are only restored via a counterattack by F/23d Infantry.

6 **c.0700hrs, February 14:** The overnight Chinese assault, having failed to puncture the US defenses, temporarily pulls back to higher ground to recuperate for the next assault.

7 **1900hrs, February 14–0700hrs, February 15:** The PVA forces deliver further preparatory bombardments, then once again launch a major effort to penetrate the US defenses, focusing on perceived weak points, especially the sectors held by G and K/23d Infantry and the French Battalion. In G/23d Infantry's sector, Chinese soldiers actually penetrate the defenses and push the 1st and 3d platoons out of their positions.

8 **1015hrs, February 15:** B/23d Infantry and Ranger elements make furious efforts to repel the Chinese from their gains within G/23d Infantry's former positions, with heavy air support, but fail to retake the objectives.

9 **1500hrs, February 15:** Task Force S and the relief formation, Task Force Crombez, fight through enemy resistance to meet up south of the village. As relief arrives, the badly mauled Chinese forces realize that Chipyong-ni is beyond their taking, and so withdraw from the battlefield.

Battlefield environment

Chipyong-ni (also given as Jipyeong-ri) is a diminutive village in Yangpyeong County, Gyeonggi Province, South Korea, 12 miles north of Yeoju. In itself, the village was unimposing, most of the population living in humble single-story dwellings made of mud, straw, and sticks, although there were more substantial brick and wood-frame buildings in the center. Its location was given significance by the crossroads at the heart of the village, the convergence of significant road routes: Route 2 to the west, Route 24 to the northeast, and Routes 24 and 24A south of the village. A single-track rail line also ran through the southern edge of the village, featuring a station and a short railroad tunnel.

From a tactical point of view, the most significant factor in defending Chipyong-ni was the presence of eight barren hills that wrapped themselves around the entire village. The immediately dominant features were Pongmi-sam to the north and Mangmi-san to the south, but the US forces labeled a number of hills for tactical purposes – clockwise from 1 o'clock: Hills 348, 506, 159, 319, 397, 129, 248, and 345. The hills varied in altitude from 328ft to 1,312ft, although their peaks were preceded by shallower ridge lines. It was

these, rather than the dominant heights, that were defended by elements of the US forces, as this defensive setup kept the total defensible perimeter to 3–4 miles, instead of the 12 miles necessary if US soldiers tried to secure the peaks.

Between the rise of the peaks and the edge of the village there were several sections of rice paddy fields; these flatter areas gave the US troops some more open fields of fire against attacking forces, especially to the south of the village. This being said, various terrain features around Chipyong-ni presented the Chinese with opportunities to make approaches under cover or concealment, including dry river beds, sections of dense vegetation, railway cuttings and tunnels (although the US troops made special efforts to monitor and defend these), and undulations in the terrain. The nature of the surrounding terrain also presented a supply challenge for the US forces, as if the enemy captured the surrounding hills then it would be relatively easy for them to control the supply routes into the village. Routes 24 and 24A were particularly vital for the US troops, as these connected with main US logistics hubs further back and were also the routes along which US reinforcements would likely be deployed.

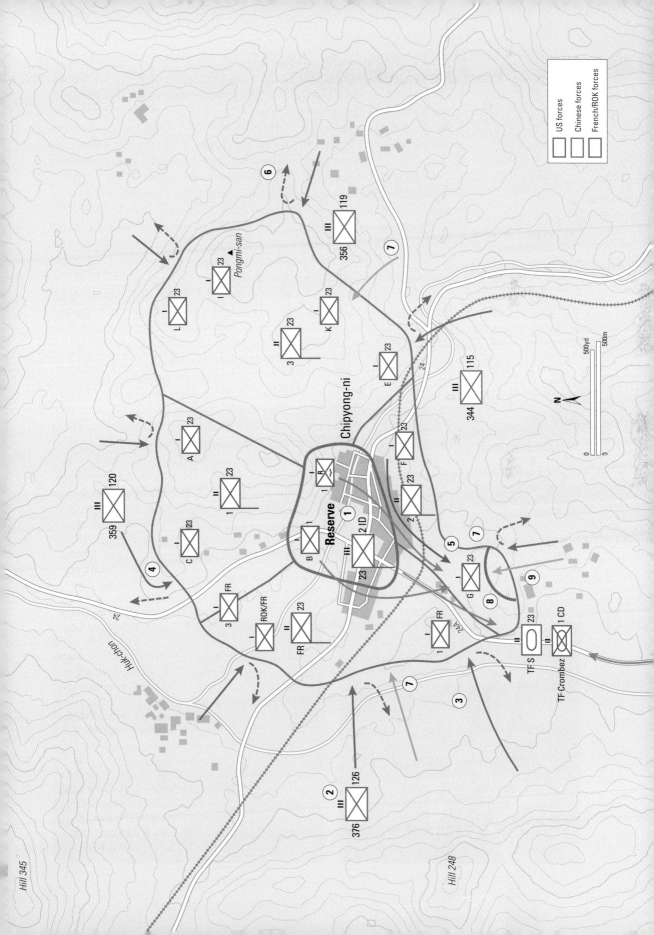

Hill 345

Hill 248

Reserve

Chipyong-ni

Pongmi-san

Hŭk-ch'on

US forces

Chinese forces

French/ROK forces

III 119 356

III 115 344

III 120 359

III 126 376

I 23 L

I 23

II 23 3 K

I 23 K

I 23 E

I 23 F

II 23 2

I 23 A

II 23 1

I 23 B

I 23 C

FR 3

ROK/FR

II 23 FR

FR 1 24

I 23 B 1

III 23 2 ID

I 23 B

I 23 G

II 23 TF S

II 1 CD TF Crombez

N

500yd
500m
0

(1) (2) (3) (4) (5) (6) (7) (7) (7) (8) (9)

INTO COMBAT

On February 12, the Chinese forces began maneuvering around Chipyong-ni, reconnoitering the outlying US positions and coordinating themselves for the eventual assault. Elements from four PVA divisions were present, and they moved through the surrounding hills until they had completely encircled the US perimeter. The PVA formations initially committed were the 359th Regiment (120th Division) to the north; 356th Regiment (119th Division) to the east; 344th Regiment (115th Division) to the south; and the 376th Regiment (126th Division) to the west.

These movements were not unknown to Freeman and his men. Aerial reconnaissance and aggressive ground reconnaissance patrols had revealed many of the Chinese start positions and avenues of approach, resulting in several significant ground engagements supported at range by the 23d RCT's 155mm howitzer assets. A small number of Chinese prisoners captured by US patrols also made it clear that a major force attack was gathering. Freeman briefed his commanders about such in the early morning hours of February 13, stating in defiant fashion: "We're surrounded, but we'll stay here and fight it out." Strict no-withdrawal orders were issued.

The battle itself began in the evening hours of February 13. Overcoming their lack of radio communications, PVA signalers sent up bright aerial flares, these marking the designated attack points around the US perimeter. Shortly after the flares went up, at 2200hrs, the PVA forces unleashed their firepower on the UNC defenders. The initial attacks were concentrated along the northwest, north, and southeast of the perimeter, and consisted of preparatory fire from small arms, heavy machine guns, mortars, and some artillery concentrations. The fire pounded the US positions, the Chinese particularly trying to seek out and destroy the 23d RCT's command post and tube artillery. Then at 2330hrs came the blasts of bugles and horns, and the expected Chinese infantry attack was launched, starting with C/23d Infantry's positions, but eventually wrapping around almost the entire US perimeter with the exception of those sections occupied by the 3/23d Infantry.

It was a chaotic, supremely violent nocturnal action, the night air ripped apart by tracer fire, constant explosions, blaring horns, and the screams of men frantically attempting to survive. During the first moments of the attack, the US forces held their fire intelligently, waiting for the PVA troops to trip flares, mines, and booby traps and so reveal their movements, rather than blaze away at the dark landscape. Between midnight and daybreak, the Chinese adjusted the pressure points of their attacks. Around 0100hrs, the 359th Regiment moved along high ground to the west to assault C/23d Infantry's flank, but was pushed back on the perimeter wire by heavier fire from artillery and M45 Quadmounts. From 0200hrs on February 14, attacks were concentrated upon the southeast perimeter, with K/23d Infantry and the French Battalion in particular battling against repeated assaults. The US troops hurled back everything they had, the .50-caliber weapons and the artillery making an especially devastating contribution, their barrels glowing hot in the darkness as Chinese casualties mounted. Elsewhere around the perimeter, there were other dramas. At one point, a Chinese company attempted to penetrate C/23d Infantry's position through a short railroad tunnel, but the attackers were mostly eliminated when US troops detonated a fougasse napalm-type booby trap in front of the tunnel entrance. G/23d Infantry was so hard hit at one point that the Chinese penetrated its sector, but reinforcements from F/23d Infantry drove the attackers back.

As dawn broke on February 14, the Chinese forces made yet more increasingly desperate attempts to drive through the US perimeter, with a concentration on the 3/23d Infantry and G/23d Infantry, the latter company in a particularly exposed and vulnerable position, requiring the intervention of F/23d Infantry to keep the Chinese from taking the positions. By around 0700hrs, however, the Chinese realized that the US and French resistance was

Shallow-scraped firing positions such as this one were extremely vulnerable to PVA fire and attack, although the .50-caliber M2HB heavy machine gun offered potent protection, with an effective range of about 2,000yd and enormous destructive effect against exposed personnel and light defenses. (Fotosearch/Stringer/Getty Images)

Soldiers of the US 1st Cavalry Division move forward behind limited armor during an assault on an enemy-held hill in Korea in February 1951. Note the soldiers trailing behind the tank in the center, using the armor as a form of mobile barrier to small-arms fire. (Underwood Archives/ Getty Images)

just too strong for the moment, and they pulled back to occupy the heights surrounding Chipyong-ni.

Freeman took stock. The US forces had taken about 100 casualties, the Chinese forces many, many more than that. Exchanges of mortar and artillery fire rumbled on throughout the day with varying intensity, but the PVA gunners' accuracy against key positions and supply dumps was improved – a blazing M16 half-track outside the 1/23d Infantry command post acted as a targeting reference point. The use of CAS was limited by the poor weather that had closed in over the battlefront. The isolated US troops did receive air-dropped resupply from US Air Force C-119 Flying Boxcars of the Far East Air Forces' Combat Cargo Command flying out of Japan, but contrary to Freeman's requests the cargo loads did not contain mortar ammunition – critical because in many cases the Chinese were too close to use field artillery – and the .30-06 ammunition was supplied in loose boxes, rather than ready-to-use clips.

By mid-afternoon, the PVA forces were ready to recommence their efforts to strangle Chipyong-ni. Artillery fire began at approximately 1900hrs, and as the night deepened the artillery and mortar barrages rippled across the US positions, with particular concentrations around the regimental command post. At around midnight, the infantry assaults began once again with renewed ferocity, falling heavily on the 2 and 3/23d Infantry. The situation soon became critical for the US defenders, especially as they were running short of ready-to-use small-arms ammunition. The French defenders performed heroic acts of resistance in their sector, including restoring their lines with a spirited bayonet charge. The Chinese, however, made penetrations of the wire at 0230hrs, February 15, against I/23d Infantry; the line was only restored in hand-to-hand fighting during a counterattack by I and L/23d Infantry.

More seriously, G and F/23d Infantry of Lieutenant Colonel James W. Edwards' 2/23d Infantry were forced off heights that screened the immediate southern approaches to Chipyong-ni. It was crucial to the integrity of the US perimeter that these positions were recovered. An initial counterattack was wiped out; then a further counterattack effort was launched around 0400hrs by a composite force made up of a Ranger platoon, a rifle platoon from F/23d Infantry, 14 men from G/23d Infantry, and three tanks, collectively commanded by Lieutenant Robert W. Curtis. Within hours, however, this force was effectively destroyed, the crests of the hills remaining in Chinese hands.

So it was that as dawn broke, Freeman (who by this time had a significant leg injury from mortar shrapnel; he would later be relieved by Colonel John H. Chiles) ordered his reserve – B/23d Infantry under Captain Sherman W. Pratt – together with the remaining men of G/23d Infantry and the Rangers to reinforce the position held by the 2/23d Infantry and to retake the Chinese-held positions. The arrival of B/23d Infantry saw two new attacks launched by the platoons of Lieutenant Richard S. Kotite and Lieutenant Maurice L. Fenderson, the first assault supported by tanks and the second by air strikes. During the second attack the two platoons made it to within 6yd of the Chinese position on the crest, exchanging grenades until they ran out, by which time Kotite's platoon was in danger of being flanked, forcing the Americans to pull back.

The US forces' attempt to retake the position finally gained traction in late afternoon, when US tanks were deployed on Route 24A to positions from which they could pound the Chinese on the slopes to the east. Artillery and terrifying napalm bombing runs by US aircraft flying CAS missions also began to smash the Chinese troops beyond functionality. (A tactical air

Three US soldiers man a .50-caliber M45 Quad Fifty machine-gun unit behind sandbags during the Korean War. The M45 was an exceptional tool for generating defensive firepower – the four M2HB heavy machine guns together had a cyclical rate of 2,300rd/min. (US Army/Getty Images)

Chipyong-ni, February 15, 1951

Chinese view: A Chinese platoon led by an NCO is positioned in a rough line behind the crest of the southern heights below Chipyong-ni, in what were formerly the positions held by G/23d Infantry. They are fighting to keep US counterattacks at bay. The center of the Chinese position is anchored by a Degtyaryov DP-28 light machine gun, manned by a machine-gunner and his assistant, empty another 47-round pan magazine as they defend their ground. The Chinese soldiers are mostly armed with old Hanyang 88 bolt-action rifles, though a couple have Type 50 submachine guns; several men are throwing stick grenades, while others are getting ready to throw their own stick grenades or hand them off to those men in a better position to do so. A few with no grenades take potshots with their rifles. Several men are wounded, one seriously. The NCO is armed with a PPS-43 submachine gun and is bellowing encouragement to his men. The Chinese soldiers are equipped with ammunition belts and bandoleers for the riflemen and ammunition-drum pouches for those armed with Type 50 submachine guns, with most of them also carrying two-cell stick-grenade pouches hung across their shoulders.

US view: A small force of 8–10 US soldiers, including an M3A1 "Grease Gun" submachine gun-wielding sergeant and a private armed with an M2 Carbine, have made it to within just a few meters of the Chinese positions, in one of several US counterattacks made during the day. They are taking cover as best they can between rough ground, shell holes, and blown-out foxholes. A number of the soldiers are throwing hand grenades at the enemy; others are firing their rifles or reloading them. The sergeant is rearing up so that he can spray the Chinese lines with his M3A1, which had a 450rpm rate of fire. The M2 had a full-auto rate of *c.*750rd/min, and its selective-fire capability has led historians to argue whether it was the United States' first assault rifle. Compact weapons such as the M2 and M3/M3A1 had particular utility once US soldiers had managed to enter enemy positions. Other members of the unit are throwing Mk 2 fragmentation grenades, which had a 4–5-second delay after pin release and a casualty-producing radius of about 15yd. Only the eventual interventions of US armor eventually managed to turn the battle in this sector in the Americans' favor.

control party was attached directly to the regimental command post.) One soldier of the 23d Infantry Regiment remembered:

> One major feeling at Chipyong-ni was the tremendous lift I got from the air force making napalm bombing and strafing runs on the surrounding hillsides. Apparently their method was to have the jets drop the napalm to flush the enemy and then the following plane would be a propeller driven unit for strafing. The jets would merely get a couple of very short bursts off during a run whereas the prop planes could fire nearly continuously and actually chase fleeing enemy. The tremendous lift in spirit mentioned above came when they were finished. They would make a very low-level "barrel-roll" run through the valley. The speed, the noise, the barrel-roll victory symbol all added to waving and indeed there was spontaneous cheering by us in the perimeter. (Combat Studies Institute 2019: 65)

Eventually, by 1630hrs, B/23d Infantry was able to ascend and reclaim the critical territory taken from G/23d Infantry.

The troops of B/23d Infantry who took the heights from the Chinese also had a further welcome sight to greet them – a column of 23 tanks and 164 supporting infantry and engineers of the US 5th Cavalry Regiment, heading along the road toward Chipyong-ni. A relief operation had been organized by Major General Bryant E. Moore, commander of IX Corps, on February 14, with the 5th Cavalry Regiment given the mission. The total relief force – known as Task Force Crombez after its commander, Colonel Marcel G. Crombez – consisted of three infantry battalions reinforced with two field-artillery battalions, two tank companies, a company of combat engineers, and a company of medics. They would have to cross 12 miles of contested territory between the US front lines and Chipyong-ni. It was slow going, with only 6 miles covered on the first day, the pace slowed by damaged or blown bridges and enemy ambushes and roadblocks. By the morning of February 15, the infantry were fighting to clear high positions to the south of Chipyong-ni, and the advance ground to a halt. To break the impasse, Crombez launched his penetrating tank–infantry force to make the final dash to reach the 23d RCT. By late afternoon Crombez's force was met on Route 24A by Task Force S, assembled by Chiles and consisting of all available tanks supported by infantry elements, and together they drove the PVA from surrounding positions in the south.

By this time, the Chinese knew that Chipyong-ni was beyond their grasp. Their best efforts had achieved little more than about 5,000 PVA casualties, against 404 UNC casualties (of whom 52 were fatalities). The exact PVA order of battle at Chipyong-ni is unclear, but it appears that at various times during the battle six regiments were thrown against the US wire: one each from the 115th, 116th, 119th, and 120th Divisions and two from the 126th Division. The exact movements of the regiments are difficult to unpick exactly, not least because attacks were often made by company-sized units (Mossman 1990: 299). Despite this overwhelming strength, the Chinese manpower was no match for the integrity of the US defense, particularly the Americans' ability to bring truly crushing volumes of firepower to bear at the right place at the right time, from both land and air.

Triangle Hill

October 14–25, 1952

BACKGROUND TO BATTLE

By June 1951, the strategic complexion of the Korean War had changed profoundly over the course of its first year. The "Fourth Phase Offensive," which had threatened to engulf Chipyong-ni, had been bludgeoned to a stop by February 20, with tens of thousands of Chinese and North Korean casualties. Stung by the number of casualties, Peng pulled his forces back north, buying time for the next offensive.

On the opposite side of the front line, there was a signal shift in UNC strategy. There was an emerging view that the war would not end up in a victorious reunification for either side, thus military force became a tool more for coercing the best negotiated outcome. For the UNC, this meant pursuing

These US soldiers are defending their vehicle convoy against communist attack, relying on the truck-mounted .50-caliber M2HB heavy machine gun to lay down heavy suppressive fire. PVA and NKPA ambushes of major supply convoys became less of a problem once the Korean War settled into relatively static lines of defense, but localized attacks on logistics runs to combat outposts remained a danger. (Pfc Sherrod/defenseimagery.mil/Wikimedia/Public Domain)

four key strands of effort. First, Ridgway's "meatgrinder" strategy aimed to inflict maximum attrition upon enemy personnel and military infrastructure, with the aim of imposing costs ultimately too great for the Chinese and North Korean forces to bear. Second, at the same time as inflicting casualties, the UNC forces would seek to limit their own, protecting troops behind a screen of firepower and avoiding the "hold at all cost" type of order. Third, operational plans would now be focused on limited objectives; offensive operations would now inch forward on a localized basis to secure the most advantageous lines, rather than make deep advances across a broad front. Finally, there was a logistical war, one in which US air power in particular sought to interdict Chinese and North Korean supply lines, further grinding down the enemy will to fight.

The new strategic foci initially paid dividends for the UNC. In February and March 1951, assorted UNC offensives brought Seoul (albeit a skeletal, shattered city) back into UN hands and established the "Kansas Line," running roughly from Paju in the west to north of the 38th Parallel above Yangyang. Not everyone was happy on the Allied side, however, not least MacArthur, whose desire to expand the war to mainland China grated publicly against the Joint Chiefs of Staff policy. Eventually enough was enough for Truman – MacArthur was relieved of his command on April 14, replaced by Ridgway, whose previous shoes as commander of EUSAK were now filled by Lieutenant General James A. Van Fleet, a hardened New Jersey-born officer fighting his third major conflict, his first being World War I.

On April 22, the PVA and NKPA launched the "Fifth Phase Offensive," a massive all-out effort to crush and encircle the UNC forces in a battle of annihilation. Ridgway knew that it was coming. The UNC forces made planned, staggered withdrawals, falling back to the "No Name Line" 25 miles farther back, while hammering the PVA/NKPA advance with heavy firepower. The PVA, its troops practically starving and with little ammunition, stopped dead at the No Name Line, and were then pushed back by a EUSAK counterattack on May 20, with the Kansas Line back in US hands by June 15. The UNC forces penetrated the lower portions of the "Iron Triangle," a crucial hub zone for communist road and rail communications, the points

ABOVE LEFT

The War of the Outposts often resembled the conditions of the Isonzo Front in World War I. In the spring months, when the thaw of winter snow rendered the trenches and bunkers deeply muddy, climbing precipitous slopes such as this one drained energy from soldiers' legs. Note the kink in the line of the trench to prevent enfilading fire. (Ed Feingersh/Michael Ochs Archives/Getty Images)

ABOVE RIGHT

The utility of light, portable small arms, such as the M1/M2 Carbine pictured, in the War of the Outposts is evident here. Dense barbed-wire defenses were of such complexity that they were almost impossible to cut, even with heavy shellfire. (Ed Feingersh/Michael Ochs Archives/Getty Images)

A US soldier cautiously probes a concealed bunker with his M1 Garand rifle while searching for hidden enemy troops. The PVA forces became masters at the construction of underground tunnels and bunkers, which they used both to sit out enemy bombardments and to make surprise counterattacks on UNC troops who thought they had successfully secured enemy positions. (Fotosearch/Getty Images)

formed by Pyonggang at the apex in the north, Cheorwon out to the west, and Kumhwa to the east.

The failed Fifth Phase Offensive was the turning point in the war. Now began the "War of the Outposts," a series of violent and intermittent clashes along a front line inscribed along and through hills, mountains, forests, ravines, and valleys with trenches, bunkers, and dug-in fighting positions, more reminiscent of World War I positional warfare. This slugging match was fought against the backdrop of ceasefire and settlement negotiations, which were moved from Kaesong to Panmunjom on October 25, 1951. The change in strategic and tactical context was embraced by the PVA. Peng felt confident that China was actually better placed than the UNC to win a war of attrition and willpower, not only on account of China's larger manpower reserves and more dismissive attitude to casualties, but also because China now had greater numbers of artillery tubes, thanks to burgeoning military trade with the Soviet Union.

By the fall of 1952, most of the front line was north of the 38th Parallel, thanks to the results of limited UNC offensives the previous May. Also in that month, command of the UNC had passed to General Mark W. Clark, the controversial former commander of the Fifth US Army and 15th Army Group during the latter stages of World War II. There had also been command changes in the PVA. Deng Hua was now Acting Commander of the PVA, with Yang Dezhi, commander of the PVA XIV Army, directing practical combat operations. The central Chinese tactic was now "active positional defense," which meant keeping US forces close (sometimes only a couple of hundred yards separated UNC and communist positions) and using artillery attrition, combined-arms assaults, and immediate counterattacks to check attempted UNC gains. In essence, all military efforts were now simply bargaining chips on the table at Panmunjom.

The battle of Triangle Hill – also known as Operation *Showdown* to the UNC and the battle of Shangganling to the Chinese – was the result of UNC efforts both to counter the pressure inflicted by the PVA's "Autumn Tactical Counterattack" campaign and to put pressure on the Chinese to resume stalled negotiations. Triangle Hill referred to a triangular-shaped elevation, the apex of its "V" known as Hill 598, located 1.2 miles north of Gimhwa-eup, just east of the center of the Kansas Line. Elements of the PVA XV Army occupied Triangle Hill, along with the nearby Sandy Ridge, Pike's Peak, Jane Russell Hill (a twin-peak feature affectionately named after the actress's physical attributes, much appreciated by the soldiery), and Sniper Ridge. Collectively, the hills formed dominant PVA strongpoints virtually atop the UNC's MLR, also acting as a protective bulwark for the communist stronghold of Osong-san (Hill 1062) 1,300yd farther to the north. US planning to take out Hill 598 began in July 1952, in the hands of Colonel Lloyd R. Moses, commander of the 31st Infantry Regiment (7th Infantry Division). The evolving plan found its way up through division and corps commands until it eventually reached Van Fleet, who on October 8 authorized Operation *Showdown*.

The overall objectives of Operation *Showdown* were to force the PVA forces from Triangle Hill and the nearby peaks, strengthening the UNC line by depriving the Chinese of observation and artillery positions and compelling them to retreat to Osong-san. The plan was fairly basic. Two battalions of the 31st Infantry Regiment would make a direct assault to take Triangle Hill and the adjacent Sandy Ridge, ultimately pushing through to Pike's Peak and Jane Russell Hill, while one battalion from the ROK 32d Infantry Regiment (ROK 2d Infantry Division) handled the easternmost objective, Sniper Ridge. Despite the very real challenges of the objectives, an almost casual optimism prevailed. Clark told the UNC command that the operation was predicted to last just five days, use only two US battalions, and would cost only 200 casualties. How wrong he would be.

A group of US soldiers gather below a bunker for a briefing, 1952. The soldier front left wears one of the early generation of ballistic vest, which protected the wearer not only against small-arms fire and shell splinters but also bayonet and dagger thrusts in close-quarters combat. (Bettmann/Getty Images)

1 October 14: After a heavy but ineffective preparatory bombardment, elements of the 31st Infantry Regiment assault Triangle Hill and Sandy Ridge, with the 3/31st Infantry driving on the center and left arm of Hill 598 while the 1/31st Infantry assaults the right arm. The 3/31st Infantry is unable to take its objectives in a frontal assault, so sends its I/31st Infantry to Sandy Ridge, which has been secured by the 1/31st Infantry, to approach Triangle Hill from the east. This effort fails in the face of heavy counterattacks mounted by two companies from the PVA 135th Regiment (45th Division). The 1/31st Infantry is compelled to fall back to holding positions.

2 October 14: The 1/31st Infantry drives through to and takes Jane Russell Hill, but four successive counterattacks by the PVA force the US battalion out of its positions.

3 October 14: On the right flank of Operation *Showdown*, the ROK 3/32d Infantry (ROK 2d Infantry Division) assaults Sniper Ridge. The ROK battalion takes both of its main objectives by 1530hrs, but a major PVA counterattack at 1900hrs results in the ROK troops being pushed off the hill. The ROK forces commit fresh resources to the battle around Sniper Ridge over the subsequent week, in a terrible struggle of attrition.

4 October 15: The PVA forces around Triangle Hill and other key locations in the sector are heavily reinforced against the UNC offensive.

5 October 15–17: The 2/31st Infantry is used to make a fresh assault on Triangle Hill. This time it takes the hill against fairly light resistance and pushes on to the base of Pike's Peak, where it is held by resistance from the PVA 134th Regiment.

6 October 15–16: A renewed attack on Jane Russell Hill by the 1/32d Infantry is pushed back on October 15 by a counterattack from the PVA 135th Regiment, but the following day the 2/17th Infantry (minus Co. F) manages to seize the position.

7 October 17–25: The 3/17th Infantry fights a bitter battle for possession of Pike's Peak, against the defense and counterattacks of the PVA 134th Regiment. Although the US forces manage to secure some footholds, Pike's Peak remains in Chinese hands on October 20, and after a lull a reinforced platoon from the 2/32d Infantry makes an advance on October 24 to within 30yd of the crest before being compelled to withdraw at 1900hrs. Another US platoon-level attack at 0400hrs on October 25 is also repelled. On the same day, the US 7th Infantry Division is relieved by the ROK 2d Infantry Division, and the battle for Triangle Hill becomes more of a Korean effort.

Battlefield environment

Triangle Hill was an excellent site for a defense. It was thickly forested, with approaches to the 1,961ft summit of Hill 598 being both steep (inclines varied from 30 to 70 degrees) and narrow. The nature of the terrain would have a particularly limiting influence upon the tactical options available to the attacking US forces. The gradients of the slopes would reduce the speed of movement for those clambering up them, the troops, heavily laden with arms and ammunition, often struggling to gain traction on the steep, gravelly ground and quickly becoming exhausted by the effort of the climb, these effects collectively reducing operational speed and tempo. Narrow avenues of approach to the summit also channeled companies into kill zones, and restricted the volume of fire that could be generated in the assault, by limiting the frontage of infantry. There was cover and concealment available, in the form of rocks, trees, and clefts in the slopes, rocks, and trees, although the tree cover was increasingly thinned out by shellfire.

Two ridgelines extended out from Triangle Hill. One went out to Pike's Peak about 1,000yd to the northwest. The other extended to the east and formed Sandy Ridge, with the twin peaks of Jane Russell Hill sitting about 550yd to the north of this ridge. Sniper Ridge sat across the valley to the east, about 600yd from Jane Russell Hill. The PVA, predicting the likelihood of an attack, had worked hard to make the landscape deeply defensible, with thousands of yards of labyrinthine tunnel and trench networks, a proliferation of obstacles, including barbed wire and minefields, and preregistered artillery support. They also had the advantages that come from elevated positions of defense, especially good observation over surrounding terrain (particularly to the south), easier weapon sighting on enemies coming up the slopes, and the fact that grenades would roll down the slopes when thrown. For the US tactical commanders, the terrain was especially challenging because it provided no avenues of approach with adequate cover and concealment, nor was there any way in which the enemy could be outflanked. Because of these restrictions, the US attack was primarily going to be a frontal assault relying on sheer firepower to provide the cover for movement.

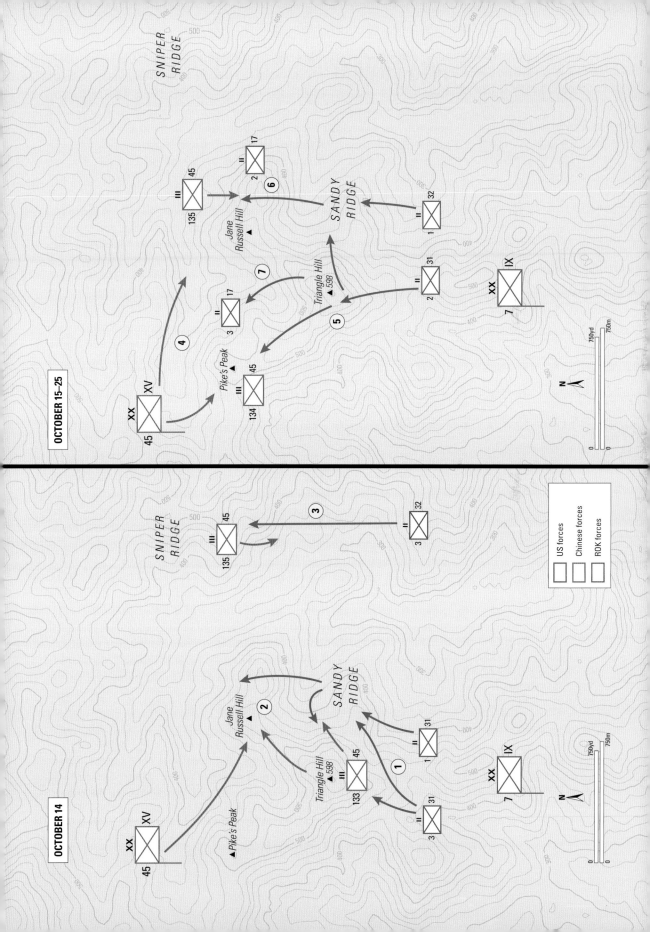

OCTOBER 15–25

SNIPER RIDGE

III 45 135

Jane Russell Hill ▲

II 17 2 ⑥

III 45 17 3

XV XX 45

▲ Pike's Peak

④

III 134 45

⑦

SANDY RIDGE

Triangle Hill ▲ 598

⑤

II 31 2

II 32 1

IX XX 7

N

750yd
750m

OCTOBER 14

SNIPER RIDGE

III 45 135

③

II 32 3

Jane Russell Hill ▲

② ▲ Pike's Peak

XV XX 45

SANDY RIDGE

Triangle Hill ▲ 598

III 133 45

① ②

II 31 1

II 31 3

IX XX 7

N

750yd
750m

US forces ☐

Chinese forces ☐

ROK forces ☐

INTO COMBAT

Operation *Showdown* was initiated on October 14, 1952. The prelude to the infantry assaults was a predawn artillery bombardment of unsparing intensity – more than 24,000 US shells would be fired on the first day alone – but attrition was limited by the fact that PVA troops took refuge in their underground tunnel complexes. For the assault on Triangle Hill, the 1/31st Infantry (Lieutenant Colonel Myron McClure) assaulted the right arm of Triangle Hill, while the sector encompassing Hill 598 and the left arm of Triangle Hill was the responsibility of the 3/31st Infantry. The PVA defenders were men of the 135th Regiment (45th Division).

The attack quickly devolved into an agony of slow movement, the US forces scrambling up gravelly slopes while the PVA troops poured down fire and explosives without ceasing. Despite heroic efforts, soldiers of the 3/31st Infantry were simply unable to approach the summit of Hill 598 and suffered appalling casualties. Attempting to circumvent the opposition, the 3/31st Infantry eventually detached Co. I and sent it to Sandy Ridge, which had been secured by the 1/31st Infantry. I/31st Infantry then made a push on Triangle Hill from the east, but the obdurate Chinese defenders, backed by escalating poundings of artillery fire, forced the company back. By the evening of the first day, the 3/31st Infantry was essentially forced back to its start lines.

The 1/31st Infantry was also finding the going tortuous. Its attack was spearheaded by a reinforced Co. A, with B and C/31st Infantry in reserve. Sandy Ridge was occupied, but as A/31st Infantry stalled, the reserve companies were committed in the attempt to break through to Jane Russell Hill. Both of these US Army companies surmounted the hill, but then faced four hammer-blow counterattacks, including a terrifying incident in which Chinese troops ran through their own shredding artillery barrage to fight the US soldiers hand-to-hand. In the end, the 1/31st Infantry was compelled to pull back from Jane Russell Hill and Sandy Ridge, at 2045hrs.

Also on October 14, troops from the ROK 3/32d Infantry (ROK 2d Infantry Division) made a powerful push against Sniper Ridge. The Koreans' experience was similar to that of the 1/31st Infantry. Having seized their given objectives by 1530hrs in the teeth of a stinging defense mounted by the PVA 133d Regiment, the ROK forces were subsequently driven from the ridge by mass counterattacks and especially brutal close-quarters fighting. (Although the efforts of the ROK forces in the battle are not the focus of this book, we should note that alongside the US engagements was an equally grueling battle conducted by the ROK, at astonishingly high cost.)

On October 15, recriminations and replanning began at the 7th Infantry Division's headquarters. The divisional commander, Major General Wayne C. Smith, committed fresh forces: Major Seymour L. Goldberg's 1/32d Infantry was assigned to 31st Infantry Regiment operational control and tasked to attack Sandy Ridge and Jane Russell Hill, while Major Warren B. Phillips' 2/31st Infantry was to have a crack at Hill 598. The day did seem to bring a change in US fortunes. Hill 598 was taken by E/31st Infantry against surprisingly minimal

Ralph E. Pomeroy

Born in Quinwood, West Virginia, on March 26, 1930, Ralph Eugene Pomeroy entered the US Army on October 17, 1951. After completion of his training on Hawaii he was sent to serve in the Korean War as a member of the 31st Infantry Regiment (7th Infantry Division). Private First Class Pomeroy's life would end, at the age of 22, on October 15, 1952, at the battle of Triangle Hill, but his actions as a machine-gunner with E/31st Infantry resulted in the subsequent posthumous award of the Medal of Honor. His citation describes the events behind the decision: "When the enemy attacked through a ravine leading directly to his firing position, he immediately opened fire on the advancing troops inflicting a heavy toll in casualties and blunting the assault. At this juncture the enemy directed intense concentrations of artillery and mortar fire on his position in an attempt to neutralize his gun. Despite withering fire and bursting shells, he maintained his heroic stand and poured crippling fire into the ranks of the hostile force until a mortar burst severely wounded him and rendered the gun mount inoperable. Quickly removing the hot, heavy weapon, he cradled it in his arms and, moving forward with grim determination, raked the attacking forces with a hail of fire. Although wounded a second time he pursued his relentless course until his ammunition was expended within 10 feet of the foe and then, using the machine gun as a club, he courageously closed with the enemy in hand-to-hand combat until mortally wounded."

resistance, after which the company advanced to the base of Pike's Peak, while F/31st Infantry swung right to move onto Sandy Ridge. Goldberg's 1/32d Infantry initially seemed to have similar success, making a good advance toward Jane Russell Hill in a column of companies, but then a counterattack from a reinforced battalion of the PVA 135th Regiment forced the US battalion into a withdrawal.

Over the next two days, the resilience of the PVA was amply demonstrated. On October 16, the US 32d Infantry Regiment, reinforced by the 2/17th Infantry, managed to surge forward and take Jane Russell Hill, but Pike's Peak, defended by the PVA 134th Regiment (45th Division), proved to be a far more difficult prospect. On October 17, the 3/17th Infantry managed to get its Co. L to the top of the peak, but further assaults by I/17th Infantry ground to a halt in the face of astonishing levels of PVA small-arms and artillery firepower at close quarters.

Hu Xiudao

Hu Xiudao was born in 1931 into a poor farming community in Jintang County, Sichuan Province, China, and volunteered for the PVA in June 1951, serving with the 5th Company, 91st Regiment (31st Division, XII Army). In October 1952, Hu found himself defending the heights around Triangle Hill against the US onslaught, notably the first time the young soldier had actually used live ammunition. He fought tirelessly, relying heavily on grenades to repel enemy advances. Hu became famous in China for his single-handed defense of one position, Chinese media declaring that he had personally repelled 41 attacks and killed no fewer than 280 UNC soldiers in one day alone. (To provide some context to these figures, the PVA estimated that it had inflicted 25,498 casualties during the battle of Triangle Hill, as opposed to the 6,229 casualties declared by the UNC.) Regardless of the reality of the figures, Hu was certainly a stoical and committed fighter, and on June 1, 1953, he was awarded the title of "First Class Fighting Hero." Subsequent awards from the Democratic People's Republic of Korea included "Hero of the Democratic People's Republic of Korea," as well as the "First Class National Flag Medal" and the "Gold Star Medal." Hu's military career continued for many years after the Korean War, and he died in Nanjing on March 13, 2002.

Hill 598, October 14, 1952

Three rifle companies of Lieutenant Colonel Myron McClure's 1/31st Infantry were challenged with seizing Sandy Ridge, while Major Robert H. Newberry's 3/31st Infantry would tackle Hill 598. First to move out was L/31st Infantry, led by First Lieutenant Bernard T. Brooks, followed by K/31st Infantry under the command of First Lieutenant Charles L. Martin; I/31st Infantry, commanded by Captain Max R. Stover, would stay in reserve. The assault by L/31st Infantry quickly ran into a wall-like defense; Brooks urged his platoons forward up the slope, but they were subjected to a rain of hand grenades, Bangalore torpedoes, shaped charges, and even rocks, thrown by weaponless defenders from their strongpoint on Hill 598's upper slopes. The above-ground fortifications of the defenders (the 8th and 9th companies of the PVA 135th Regiment) were obliterated by the preparatory bombardment, as were all radio and telephone communications, but the entrenchments and the network of bunkers and underground tunnels that supported the fortifications remained operational. The 31st Infantry Regiment was among the very first US Army units to be issued with the new M1952 ballistic vests, but the casualties among soldiers of L/31st Infantry, its lead company, were devastating. Both K and I/31st Infantry would follow on, and would fare scarcely any better.

Here we see a platoon of Brooks' L/31st Infantry struggling up a steep slope. Some men have paused to take aim and fire at their tormentors, while others are scrambling up the slope; one or two more have hunkered down in dead ground or behind outcrops of rock for cover. In the close foreground, an exasperated sergeant is pulling on the collar of an exhausted M1919A6 machine-gunner, encouraging him and his tardy assistant to keep moving up the hill where they are needed. In the center of the scene is the platoon officer, a young second lieutenant who has been badly knocked about by explosions and is now bleeding from multiple small wounds as well as being concussed. He holds his helmet in one hand, his M2 Carbine in the other, as he struggles to regain his composure and continue with the attack.

October 19, the fifth day of the battle of Triangle Hill, was pivotal for the overall direction of this increasingly desperate clash. From one perspective, the battle appeared to be slipping out of the PVA's grip – over the course of five days, the PVA had lost control of 14 out of 16 positions between Jane Russell Hill and Pike's Peak (Gibby 2017: 73–74). At the same time, however, the PVA was strengthening itself both to resist further UNC advances and to maintain a cycle of counterattacks. Qin Jiwei, commander of the PVA XV Army, had heavily reinforced the Chinese positions, using his tunnel network to push men forward out of sight and under cover. Indeed, on October 20 Deng Hua stated: "Although our hills and positions have been turned into torched soil, our troops are still holding their tunnels. Our forces staying inside tunnels have not only made facilitation to our counterattack operations but also have made independent assaults on the enemy" (AMS: 617). In short, if Triangle Hill was a battle of attrition, the PVA was confident that it could sustain it.

Proof of the PVA resilience came in the early evening of October 19 in the shape of an assault against US gains on Pike's Peak conducted by two companies of the PVA 134th Regiment. The action, like so many others in the battle, descended into desperate hand-to-hand fighting in the confines of trenches and bunkers. Bayonets, daggers, submachine guns, combat shotguns, pistols, grenades, clubs, even fists, became the most valuable tools in the dreadful scramble for survival. The weight of numbers on the PVA side, however, proved too much for L/17th Infantry to restrain, and the US company began to fall back toward Hill 598, the Chinese forces once again taking full possession of Pike's Peak and moving purposefully toward Hill 598. Reinforcements from the US 17th and 32d Infantry regiments were rushed into the sector to stop the PVA tide, the counterattacks augmented by particularly bludgeoning US artillery fire directed along the routes between

Hill 598 and Pike's Peak. Eventually, at about 0600hrs on October 20, the Chinese advance on Hill 598 was stopped and reversed. In the days immediately following, the 1st and 3d battalions, 32d Infantry Regiment, relieved the troops of the 17th Infantry Regiment, while the 2/32d Infantry relieved soldiers on the left arm of Triangle Hill.

During the following two days, the intensity of fighting dropped as both sides licked their wounds. It was a temporary pause, however. On October 23, elements from the PVA 45th Division, up to six companies strong, hurled themselves again at Triangle Hill following a one-hour preparatory artillery barrage. US Army soldiers of F/32d Infantry valiantly held their positions, albeit with reinforcement from G/32d Infantry. A coterminous Chinese attack against Jane Russell Hill was also rebuffed.

On October 25, the US 7th Infantry Division was relieved in the entire Triangle Hill sector by the ROK 2d Infantry Division. (The subsequent phase of the battle was largely a Korean affair, albeit under overall US control, so is largely beyond the remit of our analysis here.) As the 7th Infantry Division pulled out of the line, it was faced with a sobering reality. Instead of fighting a five-day, two-battalion action costing 200 casualties, as Clark had predicted, the division had endured 12 days of combat that drew in eight battalions and cost more than 2,000 casualties. Most galling, the battle for Triangle Hill was still a long way from over. In subsequent weeks, ROK and PVA forces continued to shed their blood in huge quantities in a struggle for the same positions over which the US forces had fought. In the end, the Chinese willingness to embrace attrition's logic paid off for the PVA: counterattacks pushed UNC troops from Hill 598 and Jane Russell Hill by November 1, the day on which the PVA 91st Regiment, 31st Division arrived in the sector as further reinforcement. Horrifying to-and-fro combat over Sniper Ridge continued for more than three weeks.

ABOVE LEFT
With fanatical commitment, PVA infantry at the battle of Triangle Hill, their grenades used up (note the empty grenade box), resort to throwing large rocks down the slopes at the attacking US infantry. While not an effective tactic, such actions provided ideal Chinese propaganda content. (Unknown/Wikimedia/Public Domain)

ABOVE RIGHT
US soldiers lay down grazing fire from their .30-caliber Browning M1919A4 light machine gun during the summer months of 1952. While reliable, the M1919A4 was not entirely satisfactory as a light machine gun; it had a high profile on its tripod, and was heavy to move and slow to set up. The .30-caliber Browning M1919A6, also used in Korea, was an imperfect attempt to address these flaws. (PhotoQuest/Getty Images)

A Chinese POW is questioned by US intelligence personnel before he is transferred to a prison camp. The conditions of exchange of POWs on both sides became a fraught negotiating point at Panmunjom. (PhotoQuest/ Getty Images)

On November 28, Van Fleet called off Operation *Showdown*, six weeks after it began. As the commanders took stock, there was the realization, more terrible for the UNC, that the final positions held at the end of November were essentially the same as those held at the beginning of the action. Clark explained that he considered the losses far exceeded the value of the gains, and declared the operation "unsuccessful" (Clark 1954: 79).

A US soldier uses a flamethrower on an enemy bunker. The flamethrower was a highly effective tool in Korea. The threat posed to those on the receiving end was not just the searching flames, but also the sudden oxygen depletion in the confined space. (Keystone/ Getty Images)

Pork Chop Hill

July 6–11, 1953

BACKGROUND TO BATTLE

The US forces stationed on the MLR during the winter of 1952–53 breathed the thick air of futility. Throughout history, military forces have fought for the most anonymous patches of land, many without names until operational requirements gave them such; but often such land had a value in the overall tactical and strategic context, being an offensive jumping-off point, a route to a critical objective on or over the horizon, or a defensive barrier protecting something valuable to the army's rear. The War of the Outposts, however, often came with sense of disconnection between the cost in human lives, the uninspiring scraps of land over which the blood was spilled, and the sketchy war aims. Both sides were getting weary.

Two major changes at the top changed the overall strategic direction. The first came in November 1952, when Dwight D. Eisenhower was elected as US president; the second came with the death of the fearsome Soviet leader Joseph Stalin on March 5, 1953. Eisenhower's appointment did not mean a "dove" entered the White House – he was one of the greatest of the United States' old warriors, after all – but he was nevertheless focused on extracting the country from the Korean mire, and avoiding escalation. He was helped in this goal by Stalin's demise, as the subsequent Soviet administration, imperfectly headed by Georgi M. Malenkov, was more receptive to the idea of peace in East Asia, and peace negotiations soon resumed after a six-month recess. Not that any of this brought peace on the ground, however. Fighting continued along the length of the MLR, not least around Hill 255, better known to US troops, on account of its shape, as Pork Chop Hill.

Back in June 1952, the US 45th Infantry Division, located on the right of I Corps in west-central Korea, seized a series of six key positions in front of the

MLR from the PVA 39th Army. The positions included Pork Chop Hill and nearby Old Baldy (Hill 266, to the west-southwest of Pork Chop Hill), previously defended by the PVA 116th Division. The US troops dug in and held on to their gains against the inevitable PVA counterattacks. With the attacks repelled, the US forces then made improvements to the defenses, in the justified expectation of further Chinese assaults, and the 7th Infantry Division took over responsibility for the sector in late 1952.

For the PVA, Pork Chop Hill was like a thorn in its side, and over the winter of 1952–53 Peng moved two armies into the sector. The next major PVA onslaught in the sector came on March 23, 1953, with a two-division attack against Pork Chop Hill and Old Baldy. In a brutal fight, Old Baldy was seized by the PVA 423d Regiment (141st Division). Yet again, Pork Chop Hill held out against unequal odds, but only just. A partially successfully defense did not count as a US victory, however, and the loss of a key position was a demoralizing slap in the face for the 7th Infantry Division, which became the focus of public criticism, the adverse comments repeated with much glee over the battlefield tannoys by English-speaking PVA propaganda officers – but the fight for Pork Chop Hill was a long way from being over.

On April 16, Pork Chop Hill was manned by two platoons of E/31st Infantry. Shortly before midnight, the darkness on the hill suddenly came alive as a nighttime attack was mounted by a battalion of the PVA 201st Regiment alongside attacks across other points in the sector. It was the beginning of an action so legendary that it would later be immortalized in the 1959 film *Pork Chop Hill*. The hill was retained by US forces only with the most exceptional sacrifice. For example, K/31st Infantry (the primary focus of the aforementioned film) launched a counterattack with 135 men; by the end of the engagement only ten of those men remained unharmed. The battle was a chaotic mess of close-quarters combat conducted within trenches and bunkers amid the incessant pounding of artillery fire – Pork Chop Hill received an estimated total of 80,000 rounds of artillery fire during the battle. With the application of astonishing firepower and repeated counterattacks conducted by the 17th Infantry Regiment, US forces hung onto Pork Chop Hill by their fingernails, the PVA forces pulling back on April 18.

It was clear that the blasted defenses of Pork Chop Hill would need substantial rebuilding after the battle. As an engineer, Major General Arthur G. Trudeau, commander of the 7th Infantry Division, drew up a list of necessary improvements. These included: the careful selection and development of new fighting positions to provide an all-around defense; the digging of trench systems better able to resist artillery fire and enfilading fire; the pre-sighting of automatic weapons to protect the flanks of the hill; the construction of protected and concealed bunkers; setting an outer barrier of barbed wire beyond infantry grenade-throwing range; improved distribution and storage of ammunition; more accurate records of minefields; and an improvement in the integrity of the access road running up from the adjacent Hill 200 (McWilliams 2015: 167–68).

The task of carrying out the work was given to the 13th Engineer Battalion, supported by Korean laborers. This was no conventional building project, however. The work was harassed constantly by PVA

artillery and mortars, leading to inevitable corner cutting. Also, PVA intelligence personnel kept a close watch on the work as it proceeded, identifying key points of weakness and integrating those into their plans, for since May the PVA had been massing forces around Pork Chop Hill. The core formation by May 1953 was the 200th Regiment, with the battle-weary 201st Regiment in reserve, bolstered by further elements of the PVA 1st Army.

Throughout and beyond May, Chinese activity along the entire front line began to intensify dramatically, with a significant increase in localized offensives conducted by formations up to regimental size. In the 7th Infantry Division's sector, this included a short assault on Pork Chop Hill itself on May 8, held off by E/31st Infantry, plus a US action to clear the "Rat's Nest" cave and tunnel network some 500yd north of Pork Chop Hill. There were also constant minor actions: probing attacks, patrol contacts, artillery exchanges, air strikes. It was clear that the front was about to experience another major battle. Indeed, back in April, US intelligence assessments – subsequently proving to be superbly accurate – indicated that the 7th Infantry Division would likely experience a Chinese offensive on July 6.

By the beginning of July 1953, Pork Chop Hill was held by A/17th Infantry. This relatively small and isolated force was commanded, temporarily, by First Lieutenant Alton McElfresh, Jr. On the adjacent Hill 200 was the reserve force, B/17th Infantry. The defenses on Pork Chop Hill had been considerably upgraded since the April battle, but experience had shown that even the strongest outposts could be overrun by the PVA. Thus as dawn broke on July 6, the soldiers of A/17th Infantry were on high alert.

The US Army often worked closely with the ROK armed forces in developing defensive positions. Here personnel of the Korean Service Corps unload logs from an M39 Armored Utility Vehicle at the US 2d Infantry Division supply point on Old Baldy near Cheorwon. (SFC Charles M. Roberts/Wikimedia/Public Domain)

MAP KEY

1 **2225hrs, July 6:** While occupying Pork Chop Hill, A/17th Infantry comes under heavy bombardment from PVA artillery, followed within 10 minutes by a massed attack from a reinforced PVA battalion. In ferocious fighting, the PVA forces make penetrations around most of the defensive perimeter, but Co. A manages to retain significant portions of the trenches and bunkers. This attack is just the first of multiple PVA assaults on Pork Chop Hill, occurring on a daily basis until July 11.

2 **2308hrs, July 6:** The 17th Infantry Regiment commits the first of its reserves to Pork Chop Hill. B/17th Infantry advances from Hill 200, arriving at Pork Chop Hill at 0037hrs on July 7 and going into an immediate counterattack, with heavy fighting on the right "finger" of the hill. B/17th Infantry helps the survivors of A/17th Infantry to clear many trenches, but suffers heavy casualties in the process.

3 **0348hrs, July 7:** E/32d Infantry deploys onto Pork Chop Hill to bolster the defenders there against repeated PVA assaults. By late afternoon PVA forces hold much of the western sector of the hill, while US troops hold the center and the eastern sectors.

4 **Evening, July 7:** The 13th Engineer Battalion begins the construction of a Bailey bridge over the river to the south of the battlefield, to ensure the smooth flow of US logistics to the front line.

5 **0135hrs, July 8:** F/32d Infantry deploys from Hill 347 and makes a counterattack on Pork Chop Hill along Brinson Finger. The company assaults toward the peak's crest, but is eventually stopped owing to mounting casualties and shortages of ammunition. By 0425hrs it is surrounded by the enemy and is ordered to withdraw.

6 **1540hrs, July 8:** The 2/17th Infantry makes a two-company counterattack, with E and G/17th Infantry assaulting from different angles of approach. By early evening, however, both attacks have stalled with heavy casualties while the PVA continues pouring in soldiers. F/17th Infantry begins an assault on the southern slopes at 1730hrs to reinforce the attack.

7 **0415hrs, July 9:** Two companies of the 3/17th Infantry mount a counterattack up the southern slopes of Pork Chop Hill, with the aim of clearing the eastern shoulder and the main crest of the hill. Despite making good initial progress, once again the attack stalls within a few hours of fighting.

8 **0459hrs, July 9:** C/17th Infantry adds to the counterattack efforts, driving into the southeast corner of the US positions, assaulting in APCs rather than on foot. The company manages to clear most of the PVA from the right "finger" of Pork Chop Hill.

9 **July 9–11:** Throughout the night of July 9–10, the PVA forces make further major assaults on Pork Chop Hill, threatening US positions. On July 10–11 the 32d Infantry Regiment relieves the 17th Infantry Regiment, but on July 11 all the US forces are finally withdrawn from the hill.

Battlefield environment

In July 1953, Pork Chop Hill was a blasted and bare elevation, its peak 980ft above sea level. Officially designated Hill 255, Pork Chop Hill was so called on account of its distinctive shape, with the summit to the west sloping down to the "bone" of the chop to the east, known as Brinson Finger. To the immediate east of Pork Chop Hill was Hill 200, a feature that would be vital to the development of the battles. Not only did Hill 200 provide a location for reserve forces, but Pork Chop Hill's only access road tracked the base of Hill 200 before running up Pork Chop Hill. On Pork Chop Hill itself, the access road formed a loop near the summit, the loop forming an evacuation landing area for wounded and also ensuring that vehicular traffic coming up the hill did not conflict with that going down. The US defenses on Pork Chop Hill consisted of a complex looping pattern of interconnected trenches with a total of 65 bunkers and fighting positions set evenly around the trench network, the northernmost bunkers in particular projecting out from the main trench line to give wider fields of fire against the expected direction of attack.

As with many of the battlefields of the Korean War, the landscape was a disorientating place in which to fight, especially during night actions when the heavy use of flares threw deep, moving shadows that confused visual understanding of the terrain and identification of enemy movements. The undulations of terrain on Pork Chop Hill only served to accentuate this effect and, combined with further disorientating elements such as fog and battlefield smoke from fires and artillery explosions, often reduced practical combat awareness to just a few tens of meters. The landscape in July 1953 was also deeply rutted from the artillery fire of the first battle the previous April, the shell holes providing some features in which the Chinese troops could find cover on the approach. The weather also made a contribution to the battle. Heavy monsoon rains at times masked visual and auditory signals (most useful for the attackers), made sighting and operating weapons more difficult, affected weapon performance (mortar and artillery ammunition can be particularly susceptible to wet weather), and created muddy landscape that interfered with the movement of both sides in the battle.

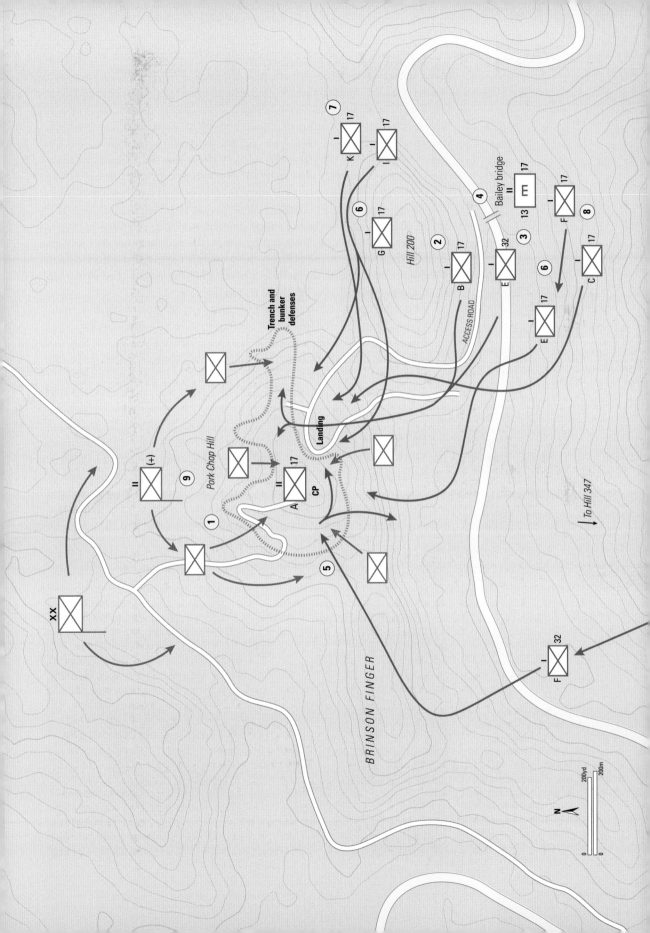

XX

II (+) 9

Pork Chop Hill

1

5

BRINSON FINGER

Trench and bunker defenses

II 17 A CP

Landing

7 K 17 I 17

6 G 17

Hill 200

B 17 2

32 E

Bailey bridge

II E 17 13 3 4

F 17 8

6

C 17

E 17 6

ACCESS ROAD

To Hill 347

F 32

N

0 200yd
0 200m

INTO COMBAT

As darkness fell on April 6, 1953, more than 700 PVA soldiers began to close on Pork Chop Hill, making approaches from almost every compass point around the base and using the cover of both darkness and heavy rainfall (it was the monsoon season) to conceal their movements from the US defenders. The first that the US soldiers knew they were about to come under attack came with a heavy artillery bombardment, which began falling at 2225hrs. This was not just a barrage concentrated on Pork Chop Hill; the PVA began firing hundreds of shells across and deep behind the MLR in the 7th Infantry Division's sector, the storm of fire intended to isolate Pork Chop Hill from reserves and resupply. Ten minutes later, the soldiers of A/17th Infantry peered through the maelstrom and saw the hundreds of Chinese troops surging up the slopes toward their positions. The young US troops were outnumbered by about five to one.

The Chinese tactic was to overwhelm the defenses with fast, mass infiltration. Notably, the first waves coming in were mainly young boys aged 12–16, armed only with grenades; it was common PVA practice for infantry to acquire their small arms by picking upon weapons dropped either by wounded or dead comrades or by enemy troops. There was method in the Chinese assault, however. Each enemy team had specifically defined bunker or trench objectives, and hit bunkers hard with flamethrowers, satchel charges, rocket launchers, and sulfur sticks, the sticks producing a choking smoke that forced US troops out into the open (McWilliams 2015: 315). The US troops opened upon with everything they had, their machine guns overheating as they delivered grazing fire into the ranks of Chinese troops in front of them. In some cases it was not enough to hold back the onslaught; the perimeter wire and the trenches were penetrated in many sectors. Platoons became separated and isolated and the company

A wounded US soldier is carried off Pork Chop Hill by two of his comrades. All are wearing body armor, and the soldiers on the far left and right are draped in M1 ammunition bandoleers, each pocket holding two five-round stripper clips. The soldier on the left also has the standard ten-pocket ammunition belt. (Bettmann/Getty Images)

command post was threatened. The fighting quickly descended into a nightmare of blades, gunfire, and screams within the trenches themselves. Even the evacuation landing area was under gunfire, and by 2300hrs Pork Chop Hill was effectively cut off.

It quickly became apparent to the leadership of the 7th Infantry Division that Pork Chop Hill would be lost without quick intervention. From 2241hrs, US artillery began slamming shells into the terrain around the hill, then at 2308hrs B/17th Infantry began advancing up the slopes of the hill, going into combat there shortly after midnight. The soldiers of B/17th Infantry found little but chaos on the hill, and were unable to establish effective contact with A/17th Infantry for another two hours. As B/17th Infantry sustained more and more casualties, however, it was clear that the company's efforts were not sufficient to prevent the hill from eventually falling into Chinese hands. This being said, B/17th Infantry still managed to retake multiple bunkers, cleared much of the area around the A/17th Infantry command post, and established a strong defense of the position's main supply bunker.

As the night of July 6–7 wore on, the PVA forces were unrelenting in their efforts to take Pork Chop Hill; during that one night, the PVA commanders sent in nine waves of infantry. At 0348hrs, therefore, E/32d Infantry, part of the divisional reserve, was also sent into the battle, the first elements arriving on the hill itself at 0408hrs and the company fully deployed by 0530hrs.

As the night moved toward daylight on July 7, the intensity of the fighting dropped for a few hours, with both sides exhausted after more than six hours of nonstop combat. The US soldiers on the hill used the time to enhance their defenses, especially by creating sandbagged blocking positions between Chinese- and US-held trenches. As daylight approached, the Chinese returned to the fight, focusing on the A and C/17th Infantry positions in

Forward air controllers (FACs) were embedded with US Army infantry and armor units to coordinate precise CAS in combat. Here we see a FAC on the right, conferring with the commander of an M46 Patton medium tank. (United States Air Force/ National Museum of the US Air Force/Wikimedia/Public Domain)

the western sector of Pork Chop Hill. Numbers of US troops were captured after their ammunition ran out. Such was the seriousness of the situation that Trudeau himself went up onto the hill, disguising himself as a regular soldier – a general officer would be an exceptional target for a PVA sniper. He quickly ascertained the gravity of the situation, but opted to fight back, intending to launch a counterattack to clear the Chinese from the hill.

Trudeau planned for a counterattack, to be launched at 1500hrs the following day by the 2/17th Infantry (Major John Noble). Before then, F/32d Infantry was deployed from Hill 347 to make a sweep of the south slope of Brinson Finger, then launch a counterattack on Chinese positions on the left flank. The nighttime advance to contact was particularly hard going, not least because the heavy rainfall had turned the steep slopes into mud, necessitating the use of rifle butts to provide leverage in the climb; it took five hours to cover no more than 2 miles. When the US troops reached the outer trenches, however, such was the surprise they achieved that they took enemy positions with scant resistance. Matters changed, however, as the US troops attempted to push up to the crest of the hill. They ran into blistering counterfire and heavy and accurate Chinese artillery fire, and as their own ammunition started to run out matters became critical. By 0425hrs, the US troops were surrounded by the enemy, and at that point the survivors were ordered to fight their way out and withdraw.

By daybreak on July 8, the 7th Infantry Division was fully appreciative of the seriousness of the situation. If Pork Chop Hill fell to the PVA, the Chinese forces could potentially maintain the momentum and make a more significant penetration of the MLR, compelling a wider US pullback. Therefore, the 2/17th Infantry counterattack planned for that day was crucial to the outcome of the battle. At 1540hrs, E and G/17th Infantry launched a two-pronged counterattack, with Co. G assaulting the east of the hill and Co. E going around to the western side. Notably, the company commanders had been ordered to keep their troops out of the trenches and instead focus on clearing PVA troops from the slopes and crest. By this time, it should be noted, the original defenders of Pork Chop Hill, A and B/17th Infantry, had finally been evacuated from the hill, their numbers terribly depleted, their survivors numb.

When E and G/17th Infantry finally made contact with the enemy, the US troops' experience was devastating. Instead of a fast-moving sweep, they became pinned down by artillery and small-arms fire of such density that simply standing upright could be suicidal. Contrary to orders, the men understandably sought relative safety in the trenches and bunkers. Soon, both of the companies had lost most of their officers and NCOs, and the attack had stalled by 1800hrs. In an attempt to inject some momentum into the attack, F/17th Infantry had been sent into the fray at around midday, beginning an assault up the southern slope at 1730hrs. As with the other attacks, the Co. F assault was roughly handled, being hit hard by automatic-weapons fire and showers of grenades. Again, progress eventually ground to a halt, the ranks of the company withered by casualties, and F/17th Infantry was pulled off the hill during the morning of July 9. By that time, the center and right companies of the 32d Infantry Regiment had been relieved by the Ethiopian Battalion (McWilliams 2015: 417).

The last three days of the battle of Pork Chop Hill were an exercise in bloody repetition, as the US commanders poured further reinforcements into the action, desperate to retain control of the hill. Two counterattacks were sent in on July 9. The first, in the early hours of the morning, was made by K and I/17th Infantry, with Co. K assaulting the eastern shoulder of the hill while Co. I went out to the west to support E and F/17th Infantry. Both of the counterattacking companies initially made good progress, with K/17th Infantry achieving many of its initial objectives and pushing on at daybreak to assault the crest of the hill, but the mounting US casualties eventually rendered the assault ineffective. It was estimated that by 0700hrs, 300 artillery rounds were falling on the US positions every minute (McWilliams 2015: 436). C/17th Infantry on Hill 200 was also sent forward, deploying in APCs and clearing much of the right finger of the hill – but the hill remained substantially in Chinese hands.

The PVA assaults (far too many to list here) were relentless, persisting throughout the night of July 9–10. Moreover, the PVA shelling was reaching deep into the rear of the MLR, affecting the forward deployment of US reinforcements and supplies. On July 10–11 the shattered 17th Infantry Regiment was relieved by the 32d Infantry Regiment, but the Chinese attacks kept on coming. Further counterattacks were made by I, K, and L/32d Infantry on July 10 and 11, but the unproductive losses eventually led

This dramatic image shows the harrowing experience of US troops under Chinese shellfire. The Chinese barrages rivaled, on occasions, the density of major World War II artillery bombardments. Deep bunkers and trenches, with heavy sandbagging and timber revetments, were imperative if US troops were to survive such shellfire. (Keystone/ Getty Images)

The Korean War was the first conflict in which helicopter medical evacuation became commonplace – and indeed essential in Korea's often inaccessible terrain. The helicopter here is a Sikorsky HO3S-1, operated by the US Marine Corps in a variety of operational roles, including the medical evacuation of US and UNC troops wounded in battle. (Bettmann/Getty Images)

to a key moment of decision on the part of Lieutenant General Maxwell D. Taylor, the Eighth US Army commander, and other senior US officers. Pork Chop Hill would be relinquished. Taylor later stated in a command report:

> It was obvious from the size of the enemy forces already committed that the Chinese were determined to take and occupy the position. Furthermore, it was quite possible that the enemy intended or had intended to attempt a MBP [Main Battle Position] penetration. The continued reinforcement and counterattacking on the part of friendly forces was considered fruitless in view of the expected toll of casualties and the complete loss of tactical value of Pork Chop … Since the enemy had committed elements of two regiments [the 199th and 200th of the 67th Division], and probably elements of a third regiment in his attempt to take the position, coupled with an estimated 4,000 enemy casualties, the decision was made to evacuate Pork Chop in a deliberate daylight withdrawal. (Command Report, 7th Infantry Division: 18–19)

By 0720hrs on July 11, all the US forces had been withdrawn from Pork Chop Hill. The 17th and 32d Infantry regiments had between them suffered more than 1,100 casualties. Chinese casualties were certainly greater, and are likely to be somewhere between 6,000 and 10,000, but the disproportionate figures could not mask the fact that this was a Chinese victory.

Analysis

From around mid-1951 onward, the Korean War took a form very different from the tumultuous year that had preceded it. From June 1950 until the PVA's frustrated conclusion of the Fifth Phase Offensive in May 1951, it had been a war of movement, and dramatic movement at that. Yet even before May 1951, the pendulum of movement was swinging shorter and shorter distances, eventually coming to rest in what became the positional warfare of 1951–53. In this new tactical environment, both sides were compelled to refine their approaches to fighting the war, and the three battles studied in this book reveal many of the lessons learned.

A common thread running through the Chipyong-ni, Triangle Hill, and Pork Chop Hill battles, and indeed most of those fought in the later stages of the Korean War, was that tactical innovation was hugely constrained by terrain. The path and composition of the front lines were largely dictated by topographical contours – the front lines ran along ridges, clustered atop the summits of hills and mountains, tracked rivers, and were concentrated in defensible valleys or around critical road networks or junctions. Often, as we have seen, the nature of the terrain dictated the viable lines of attack and resupply and the perimeters of defensible positions. It is notable, for example, that most of the battles studied here involved feeding platoon- and company-strength units into the action, rather than entire battalion or division deployments, because narrow approaches and steep terrain made it effectively impossible to send in anything larger. In the battles of Triangle Hill and Pork Chop Hill, for example, US companies often had to deploy in column rather than line or wedge, because the lie of the land simply did not allow for broader lateral dispersal.

Elevations also played a significant part in the three featured battles. According to military theory, the advantage in battle was usually held by those who owned the heights. Occupying defensible high ground brought several benefits: it provided the troops with a wider field of view over the surrounding landscape; it gave greater conservation of energy in battle (attacking troops had to face the physical grind of struggling up the slopes, as well as fighting); steep slopes often prevented the attackers from deploying their armor; and certain weapons' effectiveness was optimized when employed from heights – grenades, for example, would roll down the slopes and away from the defenders when thrown, whereas attackers might have their own thrown grenades roll back down on them. Both sides, however, also had to adjust to the effect inclines had on small-arms sighting; when shooting either up or down a steep slope, the tendency is for soldiers to fire high, thus aiming points had to be adjusted, with machine guns in particular having their barrels adjusted according to the angle of the slope.

While elevated defenders undoubtedly had the advantage, not everything was in their favor in Korea. For a start, the Korean landscape did not tend to coalesce around a single peak, but was rather more like stippled icing on a cake, with multiple peaks in close proximity. Thus securing one peak was rarely decisive, and often brought a unit under the artillery, mortar, or machine-gun fire of the enemy forces on nearby heights. In the battle of Triangle Hill, that clash was not simply a fight for Hill 598, but also for nearby Pike's Peak, Jane Russell Hill, and Sniper Ridge.

One lesson both sides learned during 1951–53 was the art of creating a strong 360-degree perimeter defense. Such a defense was established from several key building blocks: resilient and dense outer barriers and obstacles, both to delay and to channel attackers; well-protected fighting positions benefiting from intelligent placement and interlocking fields of fire; a sound network of interconnecting trenches; good internal communications between bunkers and positions; and fast-moving internal logistics, particularly in terms of ammunition resupply. If just one of these elements was missing, a defense could be fatally compromised.

One of the best examples of a tight defense in the Korean War is that overseen by Colonel Freeman at Chipyong-ni. He chose not to occupy the high ground around Chipyong-ni, on the basis that the US units did not have the strength to do so while the PVA did not possess the firepower or communications to utilize the high ground most effectively. Under his personal supervision, the US and French troops had several days to establish their defenses, which included:

Three US Army infantrymen, members of a light-machine-gun team, rest on the snow-covered slopes of a hillside during an assault on Chinese positions in 1951. The severe cold caused significant problems for US troops; the challenges included frost-lock on weapon bolts, rapid energy depletion in radio, flashlight, and vehicle batteries, and frostbite and hypothermia. (Corbis Historical/ Getty Images)

mutually supporting fighting positions; heavy coils of outer barbed wire; fougasse booby traps at key points of threat; minefields integrated with fields of fire; tripwire-activated flares; the improvised use of railroad ties and rice sacks to enhance bunker protection; preregistered artillery; and rationalized routes for ammunition supply and medical evacuation. Note that Freeman also ordered rehearsals of reserve forces movement in the days preceding the attack. All these preparations paid clear dividends once the PVA attack finally came.

The PVA also came to develop improved defensive thinking, a direction compelled upon the Chinese by the sheer weight of firepower that the US forces could bring to bear. The increasing availability of Chinese artillery in 1951–53 meant that a PVA defense often included long-range artillery used both to weaken and also to isolate attacking forces. The PVA essentially had three tiers of firepower defense: long-range artillery hit the UNC forces at the extremity of their advance, or targeted reinforcements or resupply; mortars pounded the attackers at medium range during the attack; and grenades and small arms were the main tools at ranges up to a few hundred yards. Chinese field fortifications also developed in sophistication. From the outset of their involvement in the Korean War, the PVA demonstrated competence in constructing deep-dug bunkers and fighting positions with strong overheard cover and terrain-blending camouflage, connected by zigzagged trenches to prevent enfilade fire by the UNC forces. As the war progressed, these defensive arrangements were significantly enhanced. There was a much greater use of outer obstacles, especially barbed wire and minefields. The salient innovation was in the use of extensive underground tunnel networks, some dug 20–30ft below the surface, which provided relatively safe places of movement and shelter during US artillery poundings and enabled the PVA to launch surprise counterattacks even when the UNC forces thought they had secured a position.

Offensively, both sides also innovated as the Korean War progressed, but in many ways these innovations were more limited, not least because of the constraints imposed by the nature of the terrain, as acknowledged above. The US Army almost always brought firepower superiority to any fight, and this was key to its offensive tactics. Sheer weight of artillery and machine-gun fire could smash both men and positions, and provide the attacking infantry with a stormy shield behind which they could

These two PVA prisoners have the PLA quilted cotton winter uniform, which was usually worn over the top of the summer uniform. The uniform was certainly warm, but it was hard to dry out once wet. They also have fur- or pile-lined winter hats with earflaps, but appear to have lost their fur-lined gloves, which had a separate trigger finger. (Otis Historical Archives, National Museum of Health and Medicine NCP 1887)

advance; but on many occasions – as exemplified by the three battles studied in this book – the action usually devolved into close-quarters fighting in confined positions, conditions that largely nullified greater US firepower advantages. The PVA commanders knew this well, thus they had an exceptionally high tolerance for casualties incurred during the effort to penetrate UNC perimeters. They also knew that the relentless waves of counterattack could have two key effects. First, they could deplete US ammunition supply. Second, they could inflict major US casualties. On several occasions in the battles studied, US forces were compelled to withdraw once their ammunition ran out and they had suffered significant force reductions. The PVA also improved its offensive tactics, learning to employ heavier preparatory artillery fire and ambush teams to interdict enemy reinforcements, and increasing the issue of submachine guns, grenades, and demolitions to specialist bunker assault units.

Where the PVA undoubtedly struggled, however, was in the realm of communications and battlefield coordination. An enlightening document in this regard is a captured Chinese after-action report/critique of the battle of Chipyong-ni, translated by US forces. In its honest analysis of PVA failings in the battle, it lists factors such as underestimating the enemy and inadequate reconnaissance, but it also enumerated major problems once battle was underway:

> 7. Officers of the middle and lower ranks were unable to take advantage of opportunities, assume initiative and coordinate their movements at the right moment. They failed to take advantage of opportunities [in] which the enemy could have been completely annihilated [...]
>
> 8. Inaccuracy of combat reports: During the course of the battle, the 343d Regiment sent in a report that it had entered CHIPYONG-NI and was organizing attacks to be launched against PONGMI-SAN, while actually it had not even crossed the railroad. Then again, the 344th Regiment falsely reported completion of the first stage, preventing the higher command from making the proper decision.
>
> 9. Interrupted and delayed communication: Division were unable to send timely situation reports to armies, and armies could not inform divisions of their intentions, thereby greatly affecting the control of the battle. For instance, an order to intercept the enemy at 1800 hours on the 15th was received by the division at 0330 hours on the 16th. The result was that troop displacements were carried out in haste. (2d Infantry Division 1951: 4)

Poor battlefield communication was a core problem within the PVA during the Korean War, and there is a clear sense of battlefield disorientation in this after-action report. It was a problem the PVA attempted to address through a mixture of tight pre-battle planning. Constant reconnaissance, via patrols and provoking defenders to open fire, provided intelligence about the enemy positions, on which basis assault teams were very closely briefed about their specific objectives. Once battle was joined, however, repetition of attack and the sheer weight of manpower fed into the action were the blunt tactical foundations, compensating for the subsequent inability of higher command to fine-tune the movements of their soldiers. As crude as this was, it often worked.

Aftermath

The second battle of Pork Chop Hill would be one of the very final combat actions of the Korean War. On July 27, 1953, an armistice agreement was finally signed between the warring sides, ending the conflict with a Korean peninsula divided at the same point as when the conflict began just over three years earlier.

For both China and the United States, the Korean War had been a laboratory in Cold War conflict. For the United States in particular, the conflict had given a sobering insight into the tactical, operational, strategic, and political realities of "limited war," a conflict in which neither side commits its full military and industrial resources, instead restraining military actions to a level sufficient to obtain a negotiated resolution. The US Army

Major General Wayne C. Smith, commander of the 7th Infantry Division, presented numerous decorations following the battle of Triangle Hill. Smith was later himself awarded the Distinguished Service Cross and the Distinguished Service Medal for his conduct during the Korean War. (Unknown/ Wikimedia/Public Domain)

October 14, 1952: ROK medical corpsmen of the aid station for the 1/31st Infantry (7th Infantry Division) assist in helping wounded infantrymen of D and L/31st Infantry following combat on Hill 598. (US Army Signal Corps Photo #1-4885-4/FEC-52-30954 (Sylvester)/Wikimedia/Public Domain)

had experience of such conflicts in its expeditionary past, but its most recent military memories were formed by the "total war" experience of World War II, in which the United States had unleashed its military might to the fullest expression possible, including the use of atomic weaponry. The context of the Korean War was radically different, however, as the post-World War II world was defined by demobilization and de-escalation, and the wariness of a regional conflict fanning out into another global war against the Soviet superpower.

The Korean War gave the US Army some invaluable military refinements, especially in the use of helicopter deployment and medical evacuation and the applications of CAS, although the US Army and the US Air Force wrestled for some time over who had authority for controlling the latter. In 1957 the US Army, conforming with general US strategic visions, largely turned away from doctrines of limited war and reorganized as the "Pentomic Army," a force configured for the emerging age of battlefield nuclear warfare and for countering the Soviet and Warsaw Pact forces in northern and eastern Europe. Notably, the Chinese PLA also began a major period of reform following the Korean War. It attempted to move beyond its guerrilla-style army, and sought to craft a more modern, professional armed services, modeled closely on Soviet forces. Innovations included introducing a professional officer corps, the reintroduction of ranks and distinctions, implementing fixed-term selective national service conscription, and giving

Mixed groups of PVA and NKPA personnel celebrate a victory in 1953. Although women did not serve in PVA combat units, they did spend time at the front lines as medical, entertainment, and propaganda personnel. (Sovfoto/Universal Images Group via Getty Images)

more weight to technical and tactical expertise, rather than focusing on political reliability (George 1967: ix).

Interestingly, however, both the United States and China ultimately ended up drawing back from many of these innovations during the 1960s. For the United States, its escalating involvement in the Vietnam War from 1954 onward showed the renewed need for conventional warfighting and for tactical skills in the emerging arena of counterinsurgency. For the PLA, the reforms it implemented began to strain at the Chinese regime's intense need for political control, and by the mid-1960s the PLA had largely "returned to many features and practices of the older revolutionary-egalitarian military model" (George 1967: ix). Thus the lessons of the Korean War circulated back into fashion and relevance. To this day, the Korean War offers numerous combat test cases for analysts and historians, showing how each combatant sought the advantage against opposing sides that were radically different in technology, tactics, ideology, and motivation.

The end for countless thousands of Chinese soldiers in the Korean War was to be killed by UNC firepower during assaults on defensive positions. On this particular casualty, note the twin pouches for two Type 23 grenades, a copy of the German M24 *Stielhandgranate*. (N.H. McMasters/defenseimagery. mil/Wikimedia/Public Domain)

UNIT ORGANIZATIONS

US Army

In addition to its three infantry regiments, the US Army infantry division had organic artillery, a tank battalion, an engineer combat battalion, and a reconnaissance company. Support elements included a medical battalion, ordnance maintenance company, and a quartermaster company. The total divisional strength of the 1948 T/O&E 7N was 18,804 men. Each of the infantry regiments had a headquarters company, a service company, three infantry battalions, a tank company, a heavy mortar company, and a medical company (Boose 2005: 19).

The US Army infantry battalion of 1950 was based upon T/O&E 7-15N of 1948. It was headed by a battalion headquarters and headquarters company, the former consisting of the commander, an executive officer, and staff (S-1, S-2, S-3, assistant S-3, and S-4), including an intelligence section, communications platoon, and a pioneer and ammunition platoon.

Each rifle battalion had three rifle companies, each composed of a headquarters section, three rifle platoons, and a weapons platoon. Based on T/O&E 7-17N of 1950, each platoon had a five-man headquarters and three nine-man rifle squads, each of which included one BAR gunner and one rifleman equipped with an M7 grenade launcher for his M1 Garand rifle, and a nine-man weapons squad equipped with an M1919A6 light machine gun and a 3.5in M20 "Super Bazooka" rocket launcher. By April 1953, the platoon headquarters had expanded to nine men, and now included an M20 with a four-man crew, while the M20 in the weapons squad had been replaced by a second M1919A6.

The infantry battalion's heavy-weapons company consisted of a company headquarters, a machine-gun platoon with four heavy machine guns and four light machine guns, a recoilless rifle platoon with four 75mm recoilless rifles, and an 81mm mortar platoon with four mortars. In September 1952 the composition of the recoilless rifle platoon was changed to two 105mm recoilless rifle sections and one 75mm recoilless rifle section.

PLA

Unlike the long-established US Army, the PLA was a force very much in the early stages of evolution, therefore it is hard to be precise in describing its unit organizations. At the beginning of the Korean War the PLA division consisted of three infantry regiments (each consisting of three battalions), a pack artillery battalion, and engineer, transport, medical, and communications companies (Griffith 1967: 131). Given that PLA formations were often understrength, and that there was little rationalization in weapons sourcing and distribution, official TO&E might bear little relation to the actual distribution of weaponry among the infantry units. This was doubly so in the PVA, which also incorporated large volumes of captured combat equipment. A big change during the Korean War, however, was that the PVA infantry battalions, regiments, and divisions began to incorporate Soviet-supplied heavy weaponry. Divisions, for example, formed artillery, armor, heavy mortar (120mm), antiaircraft, and armored-car regiments or battalions, while the provision of trucks made some divisions mechanized. For example, by 1953 the 112th Mechanized Infantry Division had the 317th Tank Self-Propelled Artillery Regiment and the 392d Artillery Regiment, in addition to its three infantry regiments.

At the smallest level of PLA/PVA organization, one particular feature deserves special mention. Infantry squads were typically arranged in three to four groups, and each group would consist of three or four men. One of the groups would be led by a "group leader" (note that there were no ranks as we would understand them, only leadership positions), another by an "assistant group leader," and the others by combat-experienced privates. Within each group, each man had responsibility for watching over the reliability and competence of the others. The "3-by-3" system undoubtedly had its origins in political monitoring, but in an army with poor or no communications it could also help with small-unit tactical control, allowing for the rapid dissemination of orders.

BIBLIOGRAPHY

1st Marine Division (1950). "1st Marine Division Special Action Report: Wonsan–Hamhung–Chosin, 8 October 1950–15 December 1950."

2d Infantry Division (1951). Annex No.1 to *Periodic Intelligence Report No. 271.*

AMS (2006). "The Unforgotten Korean War." Beijing: Academy of Military Sciences.

Andrew, Martin (2008). "Tuo Mao: the Operational History of the People's Liberation Army." Doctoral thesis. Robina, Queensland: Bond University.

Boose, Jr., Donald W. (2005). *US Army Forces in the Korean War 1950–53.* Battle Orders 11. Oxford: Osprey Publishing.

Clark, Mark (1954). *From the Danube to the Yalu.* London: George G. Harrap & Co.

Combat Studies Institute (2019a). *The 2d Infantry Division at the Battles of Wonju and Chipyong-ni, Staff Ride (Korea 1951).* Fort Leavenworth, KS: Army University Press.

Combat Studies Institute (2019b). *The Battle of Chipyong-ni, Staff Ride, Korea 1951: Study Instructions and Readings.* Fort Leavenworth, KS: Army University Press.

Crane, Conrad et al. (2019). *"Come As You Are" War: US Readiness for the Korean Conflict.* Carlisle, PA: US Army Heritage and Education Center.

Crane, Conrad et al. (2019). *Learning the Lessons of Lethality: The Army's Cycle of Basic Combat Training, 1918–2019.* Carlisle, PA: US Army Heritage and Education Center.

Crocker, Harry Martin (2002). "Chinese Intervention in the Korean War." LSU Master's Thesis. 1804. Baton Rouge, LA: Louisiana State University.

Doughty, Major Robert A. (1979). *The Evolution of US Army Tactical Doctrine, 1946–76.* Fort Leavenworth, KS: Combat Studies Institute, US Army Command and General Staff College.

George, Alexander L. (1967). *The Chinese Communist Army in Action: The Korean War and its Aftermath.* New York, NY & London: Columbia University Press.

Gibby, Bryan R. (2017. "The Battle of Shagganling, Korea, October–November 1952," *Journal of Chinese Military History* 6: 53–89.

Griffith, Samuel B. (1967). *The Chinese People's Liberation Army.* New York, NY: McGraw-Hill.

Gugeler, Russell A. (1987). *Combat Actions in Korea.* Washington, DC: US Army Center of Military History.

Hastings, Max (2000). *The Korean War.* London: Pan Books.

Hermes, Walter G. (1992). *Truce Tent and Fighting Front.* Washington, DC: US Army Center of Military History.

Keegan, John (1981). *War in Peace: an analysis of warfare since 1945.* London: Orbis.

Mahoney, Kevin (2001). *Formidable Enemies: The North Korean and Chinese Soldier in the Korean War.* Novato, CA: Presidio Press.

Malkasian, Carter (2001). *The Korean War 1950–53.* Essential Histories 8. Oxford: Osprey Publishing.

Marshall, S.L.A. (1951). *The River and the Gauntlet: The Battle of the Chongchon River, Korea 1950.* New York, NY: William Morrow.

McWilliams, Bill (2015). *On Hallowed Ground: The Last Battle for Pork Chop Hill.* New York, NY: Open Road Media.

Mossman, Billy C. (1990). *United States Army in the Korean War: Ebb and Flow, November 1950–July 1951.* Washington, DC: Center of Military History.

Stewart, Richard W., ed. (2000). *The Korean War: The Chinese Intervention, 3 November 1950–24 January 1951.* CMH Pub 19-8. Washington, DC: US Army Center of Military History.

Swearengen, Thomas F. (1978). *The World's Fighting Shotguns.* USA: Chesa Limited/TBN Enterprises.

Thomas, Nigel & Peter Abbott (1986). *The Korean War 1950–53.* Men-At-Arms 174. Oxford: Osprey Publishing.

USFK/EUSA History Office (March 1990). *USFK/EUSA Staff Ride, Read Ahead Packet, Battle of Chipyon-ni, 13–15 February 1951.* Pyeongtaek, South Korea: HQ USFK/EUSA.

US Marine Corps (1950). "1st Marine Division Special Action Report: Wonsan–Hamhung–Chosin, 8 October 1950–15 December 1950." *Historical Library.* Washington, DC: Headquarters, US Marine Corps.

Webb, William J. (2000). *Korean War: The Outbreak 27 June–15 September 1950.* CMH Pub 19-6. Washington DC: US Army Center of Military History.

Wright, Geoffrey A. (2011). "Acknowledging Experience: Pork Chop Hill and the Geography of the Korean War." *War Literature and the Arts*: https://www.wlajournal.com/wlaarchive/23_1-2/wright.pdf

INDEX